SAMMY TIPPIT: GOD'S LOVE IN ACTION

By
Sammy Tippit

As told to
JERRY JENKINS

MOODY PRESS
CHICAGO

© 1973, by
Broadman Press

MOODY PRESS PAPERBACK EDITION, 1976

ISBN: 0-8024-7510-8

Printed in the United States of America

Contents

Dedication

To my wife, Tex, who is my backbone and helpmeet, the most important human in my life. I am also indebted to James Robison who introduced me to Jesus; to Leo Humphrey who showed me how to care; and to Murray Bradfield, my associate and close friend who has been such an inspiration.

SAMMY TIPPIT

Acknowledgments

Special thanks to Richard Carey, Glenn Arnold, and Henry Roepken, unforgettable mentors. And to my wife, Dianna, for all the hours of typing and encouragement.

JERRY JENKINS

Foreword

I once asked Sammy Tippit if he had been blessed with the gift of faith. "I thought I had," he admitted, "until I ran into someone who really had." In the pulpit, Tippit is bigger than life. His booming, Southern voice cuts into men's hearts with a rare combination of authority and love.

On the street, the five-foot-nine, 175-pound Tippit all but melts into the crowd. He dresses casually. His appearance costs him the attention of adults during the first five minutes of a meeting, but after that the older generation's "amens" just keep getting louder. Sammy preaches Christ. There can be no argument with his doctrine or theology or results.

He lives what he preaches, straight from the Bible. Undoubtedly, hundreds of other Christian workers have the same burden, the same faith, the same trust, the same zeal, the same talent to move men's hearts. But few are so totally dead to self, so honored just to be used of God, or so convinced that they simply are pawns on God's chessboard. Praise God for Sammy Tippit, who will ever be embarrassed when he reads this.

JERRY JENKINS

7

1 / Jesus, If You're Real

It was the week before the 1972 Democratic National Convention, and Miami Beach crawled with radicals who quietly planned demonstrations for causes ranging from anti-war to pro-marijuana.

But I was there too, a twenty-four-year-old kid, speaking to the elite membership of the largest Kiwanis Club in the world and planning a demonstration of my own. I boasted no college degree and never had pastored a church, but God gave me the boldness to share my faith with the judges, city councilmen, police officials, politicians, and professional men who made up the Kiwanis.

"I'm often asked," I began, "to define the Jesus Movement. To me, the Jesus Movement is when Jesus moves into a person's heart and changes his life. Jesus is relevant to the drug problem. Jesus is relevant to the race problem. Jesus is relevant to the Vietnam war. Jesus is relevant to the Democratic convention. Jesus is relevant to all the problems of society.

"But," I said, "before society can be changed, people must be changed. We are challenging the next President of the United States, whoever he may be, to be committed to Jesus."

I came on pretty heavily, telling the Kiwanis that I was sick of politicians who were Christian enough to get the

9

Christian vote
tian vote.   ..ristian enough to get the unchris-

I cor   ..d my ten-minute address by explaining why
I b.   come to Miami Beach. "Since our 'God's Love in
Action' ministry began in Chicago in 1970, we've been
called Jesus Freaks, evangelical hippies, and street Christians. Actually, we are nothing but sincere young people
who have encountered Jesus Christ, the resurrected Saviour. He's changed our lives; and we're proclaiming to the
world that, regardless of the crisis, He's the answer."

To my amazement, this sophisticated audience leaped to
its feet in resounding applause. God had been glorified. It
was thrilling to know that we had some community support
as we planned to share Christ at the convention. While the
radicals planned obscenity and rebellion, "God's Love in
Action" planned to demonstrate for Jesus.

Months of planning and prayer had preceded the moving of our headquarters from Chicago to Miami. Besides
the challenge of sharing Christ at the convention, we saw
Florida as an ideal starting point for a worldwide ministry.

A few years before, I could hardly have cared less about
world evangelism. I was a stranger to the things of Christ
until I was a junior high schooler in Baton Rouge, Louisiana.

When I heard that Billy Cannon, all-America and all-pro
football player, was going to speak at church, I couldn't
wait to see him. He was my idol. I hung on his every
word, and I can still remember what he said about Christ:
"All of my trophies and awards don't amount to the worth
of a cup of coffee when compared to what Jesus Christ
means to me."

When this great athlete said, "Come and receive Christ,"
I hurried down the aisle.

The first thing the counseling pastor asked was, "Do you want to join our church by baptism?" That sounded cool. Before I knew it, I had filled out a card and had been dunked in water. I got wet, but I didn't come to know Christ. It wasn't until the summer after my junior year in high school that I again even considered God.

I had great success as an orator and debater in high school and had qualified for the 1964 international oratorical contest at the United Nations. I traveled to New York that summer with a group of about thirty students. On the way, we stopped at Gettysburg, Pennsylvania, and sang spirituals and patriotic songs at that famous battlefield. As I stood gazing at the eternal torch, I began to wonder if there was really an eternal God.

At the UN I was named the outstanding youth speaker in the South and finally in all of North America. I returned to Baton Rouge the next fall with the world by the tail. During my senior year, I traveled to several large cities in the United States to speak about world peace. I talked a great game.

It was a good year for parties, chicks, booze, or you name it. I was doing everything everyone else was doing and more. My year was exciting. I graduated among the top 3 percent in my class and excelled in the college testing exams. I ranked among the top 1 percent in the nation in math. I was offered scholarships at Harvard, Yale, and Tulane and accepted two scholarships to Louisiana State University.

My future seemed set for the next four years. I had success, popularity, a girl friend, and already I was being rushed by the LSU fraternities. But something was missing. I was empty. I had no inner peace. At times I even contemplated suicide.

Then one Sunday night I went to pick up my girl. Her father, a deacon in one of the big local churches, told us that we couldn't go out unless we went to church first. That really grossed me out. She and I had gotten drunk together just the night before, so I knew she didn't care that much for going to church. But her dad was serious, so we went.

At church I saw some of the guys who'd been bombed out of their heads at a frat party the night before. They were sitting in the back with their girl friends. This was really going to be a scene.

A soloist sang old-time Gospel songs and I didn't like it at all. But when the speaker, James Robison, stood up, I couldn't ignore him. This young guy really was excited. He was jumping all over, smiling and shouting, and really happy about his Christian life. I had seen people excited about booze and chicks and drugs, but this was the first time I had ever seen anyone who was excited about Jesus.

I began to realize that I didn't have half of what this guy had, even with all my success. I knew I needed his Christ. I had gone forward six years before and it hardly had changed my life, but I decided to give it another try.

I talked with Robison and then I prayed, "Jesus, if You're real, be real to me tonight. I'll give up anything, I'll do anything, but come into my heart and be my Lord." I didn't experience the big-time tingles or get goose bumps, and I didn't cry, but I knew for the first time that Jesus Christ was in my life. Christ had forgiven my sins. My feeling of emptiness was gone.

I realized right away that God would want me to use my speaking ability for His glory. I told James Robison that I felt a call into the ministry, but he misunderstood me. He just stood there grinning, showing me a mouthful of teeth.

"I said I feel called into the ministry," I repeated. He just kept grinning.

Finally he said, "Well, praise the Lord. If He's called you into dentistry, you be the best Christian dentist you can be." When we got our signals straight, he gave me some advice that has always stuck with me.

"Sam," he said, "Jesus didn't have to leave heaven to die for you. He chose to. He suffered and bled, was ridiculed and tortured. He gave His life for you. If He's called you to preach, you must be willing to give Him everything, regardless of the cost. Even if it means going to jail, or losing your friends, you must be willing to pay the price." Little did I know that his words were prophetic.

I knew that God was calling me, so I considered the cost and surrendered to Him. My ministry began immediately.

I was young in Christ, but I was thrilled with my Lord. I wanted to tell everyone. There were meetings every night that week at church, and a few nights later one of my buddies was there. During the invitation to receive Christ, I felt led to talk to him. Freddie was really a boozer, almost an alcoholic at seventeen.

"Freddie, I want you to know my Jesus," I said. He laughed.

"I've tried religion," he said. "It's just emotion. It'll wear off in a few weeks."

"No, Freddie," I argued. "What I've got is more than religion. I've found the true Jesus."

"Tippit," he whispered, "I'll tell you what. This weekend we're going to have a big blowout. We're going down to Grand Isle for an orgy with all the chicks you want and plenty of booze."

"No, Freddie," I said, "I've been changed. I've met Jesus."

"Bug off, Tippit. I'm not listening."

I had failed. I was hurt and discouraged.

Monday morning, Freddie called. "Sam? I got loaded at Grand Isle last night, but the whole time all I could think about was what you said. Can you come over and pray with me?"

A few minutes later Freddie and I were on our knees at his house. I was so thrilled to lead someone to Christ that I couldn't wait to tell others about Jesus. Another friend, Don, had received Christ at one of the meetings too. The three of us started meeting for prayer and going to church together.

The pastor took us under his wing for a few months and helped me grow. I got my first opportunity to preach at a nursing home where the young people put on a little service for the old folks. The only thing I knew to preach about was my own testimony. I preached it every Sunday in a different way.

From there, Freddie and Don and I developed the courage to go into nightclubs and bars to share our faith. The first time, we were scared to death. We knew a lot of people there, and our mouths seemed to be glued shut. We had a little prayer meeting in the bathroom. We came out in a few minutes, and still we just stood there unnoticed. Suddenly Freddie just shouted: "I can't hold it any longer! I've got to tell you what Jesus has done for me!"

When a couple of bouncers escorted him out, Don and I started sharing Christ with anyone who'd listen. Soon we were doing it several nights a week.

One night a local pastor came to me and said, "Sammy, I feel led of God that you should go witness for Christ in the nightclub across the river." This was a real bad place, the scene of stabbings and even bombings. I told him I didn't want to go. "But I've been praying about it," he said. "I feel led that you should go."

I said, "Well, if you feel led, then maybe *you* should go."

He asked me to pray about it, so I did. I learned that prayer can be dangerous. Sure enough, God told me to go. Fred and Don and another friend, Charlie, went with me. We just walked in and right up to the bartender, and I said, "God has laid it on our hearts to come in here and have a service."

He looked at me as if I had been drinking too much.

"What?" he said.

"God has laid it on our hearts to come in here and have a service."

He directed us to a little cubby hole in the back. Don, Freddie, and Charlie decided they should stay outside and pray while I went in to talk to the owner. I knocked hard on the door. It flew open and three men sat looking up at me. The manager, flanked by two huge bouncers, was counting money. I had hoped he would be alone. "May I help you?" he asked.

"Sir, my friends and I would like to hold a little service in your place tonight," I managed. "We'd like to tell the people about Jesus."

Six eyes glared. The manager looked at the little red Bible in my hand, then into my eyes, then back at my Bible, and finally back at me. "All right."

"All right?" I gasped.

"Yeah," he said, turning back to his money. "You can have the stage when the band takes its next break."

I walked out grinning from ear to ear, but my three buddies didn't notice. They stood there with heads bowed and eyes closed praying, "Lord, please be with Sam."

A few minutes later I was behind the microphone. We

had planned to give a few testimonies and then I was going to speak. But God just took over. The place was packed, and the smoke was thick.

"Listen," I began. "I don't know what you think about Jesus Christ." A holy hush fell over the place. "But let me tell you what Jesus has done for me." After I shared my story, we split up and started to share Christ individually.

Several people gave their hearts to Christ that night. We praised God, but decided to tell no one what had happened. We didn't want this to turn into an ego thing.

That week in church, the pastor announced that far-reaching results had begun because some young people had shared their faith at the nightclub. He said that one of the deacons had been approached at work by a man who had been there. The man knew the deacon was a Christian and asked him how to receive Christ.

That gave me the big-time tingles. It really was exciting. Romans 1:16 came to my mind: "For I am not ashamed of the gospel of Christ: for it is the power of God unto salvation."

As I looked forward to college, I prayed, "Lord, help me *never* to be ashamed." God has answered that prayer.

At Louisiana State University I found a little hill where I often prayed and studied my Bible. I called it Little Calvary. It was beautiful to spend time alone with Jesus.

As I began to spend more and more time with Him, God convicted me of several things. One was my girl friend. We still were dating, but she was turned off to Jesus. She wanted me to go back to the booze parties and the whole bit. It became a real struggle for me, and I knew I had to get away from her influence.

One night on the phone I told her that we couldn't go together anymore. Our life-styles were totally different.

"Sammy, I'll change," she promised. "I'll give my life to God."

"This is no game," I said. "If you mean that, prove it. Let's not see each other for two months. If you give your life to God, you won't go back to those parties."

We had been dating for almost a year and even had discussed marriage, so it was a tough time for me. Two weeks later she was back to the running around and partying. I was convinced that God would not bless our relationship. We were through.

In the ensuing months I developed a real hunger for the Word of God. In my loneliness I studied the Bible and memorized it more than ever   I attended meetings of the Baptist Student Union, but I wasn't getting enough Bible knowledge. I wanted to really dig in and study Scripture.

Late in the first semester I seriously considered transferring to a denominational college which offered a major in Bible. I realized that friends and family would consider the move foolhardy since I would give up a free education at a prestigious school for "religious" training.

I prayed and earnestly sought the will of God. I felt very distinctly that He wanted me to transfer. I applied to the Bible college and was accepted. With one semester of LSU behind me, I made the major move. I had no idea how I would finance my new education, but I was excited about seriously studying the Bible.

My enthusiasm quickly was quenched. At the new school, I joined some pastoral students in a jail ministry. We met for prayer in the dorm until the dorm director said we were bothering some students. I was shocked.

Some of us witnessed on the street, but we were informed

that we were embarrassing the other students who considered us "Holy Joes." They thought we were trying to be
super Christians. We just wanted to share Christ.

Soon some of my clothes were missing. Students were
stealing them just to bother me. It worked. I shouldn't
have let these things get to me, but they did.

I talked myself out of being "so radical" and quit witnessing on the street. I justified it by accepting invitations
to preach at youth revivals, but I had no power. Nothing
was happening. My Christianity was in a lukewarm state,
and I was miserable.

My father had been ailing for years with a severe arthritic
disease. When I heard that his condition was worse, I
jumped at the opportunity to leave this school. Again I
transferred, this time to Southeastern Louisiana University,
just forty miles from home. I had learned several lessons at
Bible college, many I wouldn't appreciate until later in my
ministry.

At the new school my Christianity suffered. I got in with
a bunch of nominal Christians who were hung up on the
doctrine of grace. They were into the idea that God allows
Christians freedom to live as they choose.

I didn't realize that the grace of God was not a license for
sin. I went back to social drinking, dancing, and even smok-
ing a pipe. During Bible study sessions I often related that
God was forgiving me for botching up my Christian life.

I became known in the Christian circle as "Botch." My
pipe was "Botch, Jr."

One of the more publicized names on campus that semester was "Tex." Debe Ann Sirman was a Texas girl who
capitalized on her nickname and won the race for freshman
class secretary.

When she started coming to our Bible study meetings, I

was the first person who ever sat down with her and explained what it meant to receive Jesus Christ. With my inconsistent Christian life, it was a wonder she even listened.

Thank God there were some girls in her dorm who were living examples of what I talked about. She saw only inconsistency in me. But their lives proved at least that what I was saying was true.

One night Tex went to her room and gave her life to Christ. The next day I saw in her the newness of life I had experienced at the time of my decision for Christ. It really shook me up.

She was excited and often cried when she thought of all the girl friends with whom she wanted to share Christ. I missed that excitement, that first love for Jesus. I realized that I really had blown it. I decided that the first thing I should do was to ditch all the habits I had regained.

We started to date regularly and I gave up drinking, dancing, and even Botch, Jr.—not for Tex, but to break down the barriers to sweet fellowship with my Lord. Tex and I were in love by the time I received a phone call in March of 1968. My father was dying.

I didn't even have time to tell Tex. I drove to Baton Rouge in a state of confusion, complemented by a puzzling sense of peace. I drove slowly, thinking about death, life, my father, and how I had failed him so many times.

Not many months before he had told me that he had gotten things right with God. That had thrilled me, but now I was worried.

It was four o'clock in the morning. Two aunts were sleeping in chairs by my father's hospital bed. My mother sat in the corridor. I held his hand as he first gasped for air. I shouted, "Dad!" and everyone woke up.

My mother ran into the room, crying. I saw life leave Dad's body. It hurt me to see my family go through such heartache, but I knew my father was with Christ, and that God was with me.

Back at school, Tex and I began to think about marriage. I spent more time in prayer. God had forgiven me for my stagnant Christianity and He gave me a burden for the world—not just for a few souls, but for the world.

I couldn't shake the thought that someday I would preach the claims of Christ behind the iron curtain. I felt a real desire to further His cause throughout the world, but I didn't know what I could do as a student.

I sent a little money to evangelistic concerns in iron curtain countries, but that didn't satisfy my burden. Then one day God spoke to me in a way He never had before. As I prayed, a very distinct picture came to my mind. I saw myself sitting in a glassed-in restaurant. People sat all around me, speaking in a language I didn't understand. The picture became very clear. It definitely was a vision from God. I felt He was calling me to a ministry behind the iron curtain.

I never shared the vision with anyone until after Tex and I were married. I related the story to a group of young people, who were thrilled. They wanted to have a car wash and raise money to send us overseas. They made seventy-two dollars.

After about a year, I dismissed the idea. I put the seventy-two dollars away, but I began to wonder if my vision really had been a vision after all. I badly wanted to reach people for Christ, but regardless of how I preached or witnessed, I bore no fruit. It took a fiery redhead with a heart full of love, Leo Humphrey, to turn me around.

2 / Getting in the Casket

Leo Humphrey is a muscular, stocky man in his mid-30s, a rough and tumble sort of guy you wouldn't want to fool with. He was a student at New Orleans Baptist Theological Seminary and worked with Bob Harrington, the chaplain of Bourbon Street, to share Christ in the famed French Quarter.

I'd heard that Leo was a good speaker, so I scheduled him for a meeting at Southeastern Louisiana State. I wasn't quite prepared to meet him. He didn't look like a Christian, but he didn't wait for the meeting to begin before he started witnessing to people and winning people to Christ at the university.

I was intrigued. This fireball, crackerjack Christian didn't pass anybody without telling him, "Jesus loves you!" I mean Leo talked to *everybody* about Christ. He was happy and joyful and seemed to live by the power of God. His witness was fruitful—something I couldn't say for my own. Leo was unlike anyone I had ever met, and I was determined to find out what made him tick.

I started going down to the French Quarter in my spare time to work with Leo. What blew my mind was that he didn't just witness for Christ during his working hours. He witnessed all the time. I figured it was his job. After all, he worked for Bob Harrington. But Leo shared Christ as if he would rather do that than anything else. And he would.

We stopped for coffee one evening in a little cafe in the French Quarter. Leo was jumpy. I just cooled my heels, but he went to talk to the waitress about Christ. Then he went to a back room. I sat there ordering more coffee.

A little while later, Leo came back with a big grin. "Praise God, Sam," he said. "Three of the cooks just got saved!"

I could hardly believe it. *What is it with this guy?* I thought.

Another trick of Leo's was to tell nightclub owners that he was praying for them. "I'm praying that you won't sleep until you give your heart to Jesus," he'd say. Then he'd write their names in his prayer book and walk out.

I challenged him. "Leo," I said, "you just can't witness that way. You'll turn those guys off."

But more than one came to Leo and said: "Man, would you please quit praying for me? I haven't slept for days." I was learning.

I saw Leo go up to Black Panthers, bikers, and all kinds of bad dudes, shake their hands, look them in the eye, and say, "Brother, I love you." I began to seriously wonder if he was gay. I'd never heard of a guy who told another man that he loved him.

The French Quarter really was messing my mind. I saw public immorality, kids freaking out on drugs, knife fights, and even murders. Kids talked about death like you and I would talk about the weather.

I saw runaways, teenage girls who were there just to sell their bodies. I stepped into a gay bar and saw men kissing and holding each other, dancing. I saw a world that was about to explode in its sin. It was like Sodom and Gomorrah relived.

My heart was breaking. I knew the French Quarter was

not unique in America, but I never had seen such concentrated sin. I developed a tremendous burden for a dying world. I was a college senior and doing well academically, but this burden grew. Something had to give. The sin of the French Quarter haunted me daily.

Even in class I saw kids messing up their lives. I began to pray that God would let me help people find Jesus. The burden became so strong that I couldn't stay in school. I dropped out, realizing the consequences, yet unable to sit in class when a lost world needed my Jesus.

My father's last request had been that I stay in school. My whole family was concerned about me, and it hurt them when I quit. Friends reminded me that without a college degree I would never preach in a large church or gain a ministerial reputation. And where would I go? What would I do? I didn't have any source of income. Somehow I knew that God would take care of Tex and me. I felt He led me, and I never doubted that He would provide.

Somehow, my ministerial reputation wasn't as important to me as it once had been. Though it has worked out that I have preached in some of the country's largest churches, I would be satisfied just to share Christ on the street.

Tex was beautiful about it. She said, "Sammy, wherever God calls you, I'll be with you." She has kept that spirit and has been the greatest blessing I could have asked for in my ministry.

I called Leo and told him that I wasn't going to wait for some mysterious door to open. "I want to come down and witness with you in the French Quarter," I said. Tex and I loaded everything we owned into my car and drove to Leo's office. The first real test of our faith came right away.

While we were upstairs talking to Leo for a few minutes,

our car was ransacked. There we were, two young kids with nothing but a car, a burden, and the clothes on our backs. We didn't know where we'd sleep or when we'd eat.

I wondered if I'd made a mistake, but quickly I was filled with a feeling of peace. I knew I was in God's will. He just wanted us to start from scratch.

There was an evangelism conference in progress at the Baptist seminary, so Leo signed me up and got us a room. Pastors and evangelists were there from all over the country.

I didn't have a razor or a change of clothes, so I looked pretty grubby, but I wanted to learn more about sharing Christ. The first session I went to was a discussion on what makes an evangelistic crusade successful. After hearing a lot of different ideas, some good and some not, I thought about speaking up. I wasn't sure I wanted to draw attention to myself. I was one of few people there without a coat and tie, and I had a couple days' growth on my chin.

But I finally spoke up. I told the nearly 300 pastors and evangelists that we have to take Jesus to the people and not expect them to come to Him. We have to get out on the street and present the claims of Christ to anyone who will listen.

I guess I got a little carried away. While I had the floor I took a few moments to share the burden I had received since seeing the sin and degradation of the French Quarter.

After the session, several pastors from different parts of the country crowded around and asked if I would come to their churches to speak. I was floored. God had opened the door for me to share my burden in churches all over, and I had stepped out on faith only a few days before.

The speaking engagements helped meet our financial needs, and it became exciting just to trust God when we needed money.

Tex and I moved into a house in Hammond, Louisiana, for eighty dollars a month. One night I was scheduled to speak at a church, but we didn't even have the money to put enough gas in the car to get me there. The rent was due and I needed clean clothes and a haircut, but we were flat busted. We didn't know what to do except to pray.

Tex and I knelt in our little living room and claimed the promise in Philippians 4:19, "My God shall supply all your need according to his riches in Glory by Christ Jesus." We got up, believing that God would take care of us.

I went to the post office to pick up the mail and there was a gift, a hundred-dollar check. That paid the rent, cleaned our clothes, cut my hair, put gas in the car, and even paid for a few groceries. And the speaking engagement gave us enough to live on for a while. God has met our needs so many times.

The burden grew, and I began to minister in many cities. We witnessed on the street and I preached in churches, my heart going out to unsaved people. But still I wasn't satisfied that I was doing all I could.

There was a strange lack of power in my witness. I really wasn't bearing fruit. I had a burden but no power. Again it would take Leo to head me in the right direction.

I got another chance to work with Leo Humphrey when we both were invited to a youth crusade in Gulf Shores, Alabama. I was to be the speaker and he would lead the personal evangelism. I still wasn't sure about old Leo, so I looked forward to the opportunity to really find out what he was all about.

The first night he shared with me what he'd learned from evangelists who preached with power—people like Harrington and Arthur Blessitt of California. I confided in him that I felt a lack of power, a void in my ministry.

"Sam, do you really want the power of God in your life?" he asked.

I said, "Yes, I sure do."

"Then let's go to the beach and pray about it."

We went down to the Gulf of Mexico. I had a feeling of anticipation. I was glad that I had opened up to Leo; but before we prayed, I knew I had to tell him more. "Leo," I began, "I've got to tell you something. I thought you might be a homosexual when I first worked with you."

Leo laughed. "Well, Sam," he said, "to tell you the truth, I had thoughts that you were in this whole thing for yourself."

"Sometimes I think I *am* in it for myself. But I want to get right with God and I want you to forgive me."

"Brother, I forgive you," he said. "Let's pray."

We prayed that God would empower me and multiply my ministry. Then I wandered along the beach by myself. I lay on my back in the sand and gazed at the stars. I heard the waves crashing and I was awed by God's handiwork.

"God," I prayed, "I see Your magnificent power before me, but I'm not experiencing it. I want so badly to bear fruit in my ministry. I need Your power." I poured out my heart to God, confessing my sin. He searched my heart and brought unconfessed sin to my mind. He exposed my bad attitudes, and I begged His forgiveness.

God forgave and cleansed me, and I began to thank Him. I couldn't praise Him enough. Four hours later Leo shook me. "Sam, it's four o'clock in the morning, brother. Let's go."

All I could do was praise God. I grinned at Leo. "Praise God," I said. "Praise God." Jesus had taken complete control of my life. I couldn't even sleep that night. I just kept praising God.

During that week of meetings we were to see over 130 souls saved, mostly through personal witnessing. God had given me His power.

Before the first meeting, the weather was so bad that our tent on the beach was about to be blown away. Leo said, "Guys, we aren't going to be able to hold the meeting if this weather doesn't let up. So let's ask God to stop the rain."

A few of us formed a circle inside the tent and knelt to pray. I asked God to stop the rain, but my faith was weak. I really did not expect it to stop. Somebody in that group had more faith than I did, because God stopped the rain.

Unknown to us, a girl from Louisiana stood in the back and had heard us ask God to stop the rain. She thought we'd gone nuts. She was a biker, an "old lady." She prostituted for her "old man" in the American Breed cycle gang from New Orleans.

Leo had witnessed to her in the French Quarter and had invited her to this week of meetings. She had a girl friend in one of our singing groups, and when she heard that the crusade was to be held on the beach, she decided to come.

Her name was Kelly. She'd been prostituting since she was kicked out of the house by her father when she was thirteen years old. She had seen him kill her brother with a knife. Now she was seventeen and God was speaking to her.

She had only come to get away from New Orleans for a while, and to look for some good drugs on the beach. But she sat listening to me preach that night with a lot of things on her mind. I preached on the second coming of Christ. She thought about that, and she thought about Leo and her girl friend's witnessing, and she thought about the rain stopping. But she didn't come forward to receive Christ.

After the meeting I saw her in the parking lot, standing by an old jalopy. "Kelly," I said, "Jesus loves you."

"Bug off, man," she said. "Don't give me that. If Jesus loves me, why am I strung out on dope and running with a cycle gang?"

I admitted that I didn't know. "All I know is that Jesus wants to give you a new life now," I said.

She turned and ran to the shore, calling over her shoulder, "Just leave me alone! I have to think."

Later Leo and I sat on either side of her on the beach. We talked and prayed and talked and prayed and talked and prayed for hours. Finally, at three o'clock in the morning, Kelly prayed, asking Jesus to show her His love. She asked Him to forgive her sins and to come into her heart. Then she cried and said softly, again and again, "He's real."

Kelly couldn't sleep that night. She had to tell someone what had happened, so she ran back up to the parking lot. The only person around was a middle-aged man about to get into his car. "Sir," she said, "Jesus has changed my life and now I'm a Christian."

The man looked at her like she was from another planet. She wore psychedelic pants and a sweatshirt and real heavy eye makeup. "You can't be a Christian," he said. "You're wearing eye makeup!"

She ran and washed off her makeup and hurried back. "Sir, can I tell you about Jesus now?"

The next day she went to church wearing the same clothes. They were all she had. Her girl friend told the congregation how Kelly had come to Christ. Then the pastor talked about her. After church Kelly told me, "Church was fine, but everybody talked about me except me. I wanted to tell everybody about it."

So, that night in the tent I scheduled her to speak just before my sermon. After she told about her experience with Christ, she walked out of the meeting. I wondered what was wrong. Nothing was. She had spotted two boys across the street and went to share Christ with them.

Kelly didn't have a home to go to, so for the next three months she traveled with Tex and me. During that time, I saw her personally lead over 150 kids to Christ. She went to church with us, and at the end of a service she would stand at the door to ask people if they had met the Lord.

Kelly barred no one. She asked deacons and even pastors, "Are you saved?"

She finally returned to New Orleans to finish high school. When she told her biker friends about her new life, her "old man" said, "Chick, forget about this religion. You're riding with me tonight."

She refused, telling him, "I've got Jesus and I don't want that anymore." The big, tough biker beat her up.

The next day Kelly had a black eye. "What happened to you?" I asked.

"Praise God, I got beat up for Jesus!" she said, grinning. She faced her problems and temptations and often met with failure and frustration. But she always got back up and lived for the Lord. God showed me, partly through Kelly, that His power could change lives. Now I had power to go along with the burden.

When I got back to Hammond, Louisiana, I shared with an old college buddy, Ramsey Gilchrest, what God had been doing in my life. What intrigued us both was what Leo had said about Arthur Blessitt. Arthur had a successful ministry in a building called "His Place," for dopers and hippies on the Sunset Strip in Hollywood, California. Ramsey and I decided that the best way to learn from Arthur would be to go see him. Our wives agreed.

We pooled our money, took homemade sandwiches, took turns driving, and made it to California in thirty hours.

When we arrived, Arthur had just come in from witnessing all night. He slept for two hours and then got up to talk to us. I asked him to relate some of his experiences, but Arthur just looked at me and then he said, "You've got to get right with God."

I told him that I had already gotten right with God, but he said, "You need to die daily. What you experienced the night you say you got right with God, you can experience continually if you'll die daily."

He showed me Galatians 2:20: "I am crucified with Christ: nevertheless I live; yet not I, but Christ liveth in me: and the life which I now live in the flesh I live by the faith of the Son of God, who loved me, and gave himself for me."

In Arthur's living room, a strange thing took place. Again I prayed for the power of God, but this time I placed my desires in a casket. I placed my wife in that casket along with my car and my belongings, and yes, even my desire to be another Billy Graham.

I placed all of the things I could think of in that casket, and then I hopped in and God nailed down the lid. Sammy Tippit died to self. It wasn't an emotional experience, but I knew Christ had taken over the life I had given up. Now I had Christ's control *and* the Holy Spirit's power to go along with my burden for souls.

The first thing I wanted to do was to tell someone about Jesus. We heard someone walking by outside, and Ramsey and I nearly broke the door down trying to get out there. Who should it be but the son of a rabbi from Beverly Hills. It was the first Jew I had ever witnessed to.

I told him that Jesus loved him, that He had died for him and was buried for him and arose for him. I said, "If you'll give your heart to Him, one day He'll come again for you."

"But I'm a Jew," he interrupted.

"Praise God," I said. "Jesus was a Jew." And I kept witnessing.

"I'd really like to know your Jesus," he said. We knelt and he received Christ right there.

I thought the French Quarter was bad, but the Sunset Strip really shook me up. Cycle gangs roared up and down the Strip on huge choppers. The bikers wore chains and blades. "Lord," I said, "I think I need to die to self again." I began a relationship with Christ where I learned moment by moment to yield myself to Him. That night I led four kids to Christ in "His Place."

We spent only a few days in Hollywood, but it was long enough to give me a burden to serve Christ in a large city. I felt that God was leading me to Chicago, so I started praying about it. The Lord had a lot to teach me first.

My first lesson was learned in south Louisiana. I preached in a church where revival broke out almost immediately. I had shared Kelly's testimony, and people realized that God could change anyone. Many were getting right with God.

The pastor took me aside after the first meeting and told me, "If you don't change your methods, you're going to have to leave."

I was shocked. "What do you mean?"

"You're using psychological techniques to get my people emotionally stirred."

I said, "Man, I'm just preaching the facts of God's changing power."

"And stop preaching that the church can't save a person," he said. "You and I know that it's true, but you're causing people to doubt their salvation."

"Well, I didn't intend it that way," I said. "But if they're doubting, then maybe they should be."

He laid down an ultimatum. "Change your style or leave." I told him I'd pray about it. And I did.

I seriously debated whether or not I was using the right methods. I prayed, "Lord, please show me in some way that I'm letting Your Spirit preach through me. If it's me who's doing this, then I'll quit." God had changed my life. I wasn't interested in anything big or dramatic. I just wanted to see people come to Christ in genuine commitment. I prayed that God would show me soon that I was doing the right thing.

At about two o'clock that morning I was still up, pacing and praying, seeking the will of God. The phone rang. It was the church youth director. "Sammy," he said, "revival has come."

He told me that a full-time Christian worker, with whom I had gone to college, had come to his house crying. The young man confessed: "God won't let me sleep until I return these shirts I stole from Sam when we were in college. I saw in the meeting tonight that he has something real. I was wrong to make fun of him."

That was all I needed. I knew that God blessed my preaching and that I could not change. I told the pastor the next day that I loved him and his church, but that I would have to leave the revival if I couldn't preach the way I felt led. He told me to leave. I understand that those people bugged that pastor until he baptized them.

It would have been easy for me to be bitter and turn my back on the institutionalized church, but I couldn't. God showed me during the next few days that I cannot turn my back on a Christian brother, regardless of who he is. Many people have tried to encourage me just to go off and do my own thing without the Church, but God showed me that He instituted the Church. There's no substitute for it.

I realized that if revival could come within the church, we wouldn't have to worry about the heresy that is so widespread today. God showed me that I must relate the kids to the church and the church to the kids. It's a two-way street. Kids may get saved on the street, but if they can't relate to the church they'll blow away with the wind. Many kids don't like church because too many church services are like funerals. I was burdened to see revival within the church.

God proved in a practical way what He had taught me when I was invited to speak at a week of meetings in the twin cities of Monroe and West Monroe, Louisiana, early in 1970. The experience was to become a turning point in my ministry.

3 / God Said to Walk

I had been invited to speak at Calvary Baptist Church in Monroe by Pastor L. L. Morris. I was a little hesitant about the meetings because there had been little publicity. Only four young people showed up at the prayer meeting the night before the first service.

"Wow, this is gonna be a bummer," I said. "We might as well give up if the young people aren't even interested."

But L. L. Morris wasn't a quitter. "Sammy," he said, "I believe God. Before this week is over, I believe God is going to shake Monroe for His glory, and people are going to be saved. Strange things are happening these days."

The meetings were to run from Wednesday night through Sunday. There was a fair crowd the first night and a group from Northeast Louisiana State University sang. There were a few decisions for Christ.

But the next night, I felt the presence of God in a dramatic way. During the invitation a Sunday school teacher came forward to pray with the pastor. Then he came up to the pulpit and all but pushed me aside.

"I just got on my knees and prayed for God's forgiveness," he announced. "I'm supposed to be an example to the kids in this church, but you can find booze in my icebox anytime. I've been a poor Christian, and I want you to forgive me."

The Holy Spirit came on that place. The singing group

from the university confessed that though they'd been singing for Christ, they'd fallen down in their personal witness
for Him. They committed themselves to do nothing but
glorify Jesus.

Many people came to Jesus during the next few days,
and the crowds kept getting larger. God worked like I had
never seen Him work before. By Sunday night the crowd
was so large that we decided not to close out the services.
We moved into two larger buildings.

Local college kids were asking for time in class to tell
what God had done in their lives. Ray Mears, a choir director in the local high school, shared Christ with his music
class. He couldn't give an invitation right there, so he asked
those interested in hearing more to see him after class. All
but two stayed.

We set aside a room in the local Christian coffeehouse,
"Your Place," for prayer around the clock. Pastors, laymen, women, and teens came at different times during the
day and night to pray for revival. God didn't need publicity to do His work.

We prayed that God would touch the heart of former
Louisiana Governor James Noe, owner of one of the television stations in Monroe. We prayed that he'd give us
free time to tell about the revival.

God gave us even more than we asked for. Noe gave us
all the free spot announcements we wanted and two fifteen-
minute shows besides.

"You're having trouble holding all the people, right?"
he asked. "How would you like to have the civic center?"
We nodded with our mouths hanging open, and he wheeled
around in his chair to call the mayor.

"Mayor, I want you to donate the civic center to these
boys. They're doing something positive and constructive,

so let's give it to them free. If they have to pay, I'll cover it." Praise God!

One night about midnight a girl named Connie McCartney came into "Your Place." She was stoned on speed. She had heard me at the revival, and Tex had witnessed to her; but she had shown little interest.

Connie had been raised in a Christian home and had received Christ when she was a youngster. But when she grew up and saw what the world had to offer, she rebelled and turned her back on Christ. She started doing speed when she was thirteen.

At twenty she had been to two federal narcotics hospitals and was out on a $10,000 bond when she was busted again, this time for selling. Now she was in line for a sure prison term.

"Sam," she said that night, "speed is my lover. When I wake up in the morning, I can't do anything, I can't even think without speed. I'm strung out. I've tried everything, including four psychiatrists who tell me I'm schizophrenic.

"I flunked out of college, and I'm into astrology and witchcraft. I'm a slave and I want out. Can Jesus set me free?"

It was a thrill to tell Connie, "Yes, God has promised to deliver you from anything, even speed, if you'll give Him your life. Jesus said that the truth shall make you free."

That night Connie stepped out on faith and committed her life to Christ. She's never since had a desire for dope. She went home that night and, according to Connie, flushed her drugs down the toilet in the name of the Father, the Son, and the Holy Ghost.

Another who came to Christ through the coffeehouse ministry was Joe Prophet, a Black football star from Northeast Louisiana State. I didn't even know who he was. I asked him if he'd like to talk about knowing Jesus. He said sure. After hearing the claims of Christ, he said, "You know, this is what I've been looking for for a long time."

Joe and Connie spoke at the civic center the following Friday. Joe told the crowd that sports had been his whole life. That night he was supposed to be at a track meet, but he said, "I told the coach I couldn't make it because I wanted to come here and talk about Jesus. He is first in my life now."

Keith Babs, the news director of television station KNOE, interviewed me on the evening news. "We understand something is shaking the twin city area," he said.

"Jesus is shaking it," I said. "People are finding that Jesus Christ is the only hope for the world."

I called Leo to tell him how God was blessing. "Sam," he said, "God is getting ready to do a mighty work in America. I just got a call from Arthur Blessitt on his 'Which Way America?' walk for Christ."

Leo said that at a Blessitt meeting in Albuquerque there were a thousand decisions for Christ. As I put down the phone, my heart burned to see America turn back to God. I got on my knees and asked God what I could do to glorify Him. He seemed to say, "Sammy, walk. Walk, walk, walk."

The whole idea of walking across the country sounded crazy to me. Outside of Arthur, I never had heard of anyone walking for Jesus. "God," I prayed, "I have a wife to think about. How will she react? Lord, I'll go if You want me to, but You'll have to deal with Tex and make her willing to trust You in this."

A few days later, when I finally confronted Tex with the idea, she was excited. God had spoken to her less than a half hour before, simply impressing upon her heart that she should be willing to follow Him, regardless of where He led.

"Had you come up with this idea an hour ago, I would have thought it was crazy," she admitted. "But now I'll stick with you for Jesus."

We prayed and committed our lives to the glory of Christ, still not exactly sure of what we were to do. We did know that we couldn't walk alone. God was to call five other dedicated Christians to walk with us.

When Ray Mears, the choir director, heard of our plans, he spent much time in prayer. Then he came to me. "Sam," he said, "I believe God is calling Charlotte and me to go with you."

The stakes were high for Ray and Charlotte. Ray was five credit hours away from his college degree and was $1,100 in debt. Charlotte was three months pregnant.

Ray wanted to pay off his debts before the walk, so he put his car up for sale. A car dealer told him he'd never get more than $800 for it, but Ray trusted God for $1,100. Holding out for several days, Ray finally took his car to an auction. It was sold for $1,100.

Ken Hall, a college freshman, felt God wanted him to go with us too. His decision was made difficult by his father. Mr. Hall drove up from Shreveport, Louisiana, to talk to Ken and Ray and me.

"Son," he warned, "if you leave on this walk, you may never see me alive again. I don't have long to live, and I may be dead before you return."

I figured we'd lost Ken and I was willing to let him stay, but he surprised me. He looked his father in the eye and said with conviction: "Daddy, I love you. But I love Jesus more, and I have to do what He has told me. Even if I never see you again, I have to do the will of God."

I knew Ken meant business. Later his father admitted that he'd been lying about his health.

Richard Medaries was a rock drummer who had turned his life and talent over to the Lord. God led me to approach him about the walk. Little Richard, as he came to be known, was hesitant at first. But through prayer, he felt God burdening his heart. He would bring his drums along.

And then there was Connie, the former speed freak. We knew she would have to come back to Monroe to stand trial in April, but she wanted to go anyway. She expected several years of prison, and she wanted to learn how to share her faith with other inmates.

There really was nothing exceptional about any of the seven of us, but we all wanted to be used of God.

I finally got hold of Arthur and told him our plans. We had decided to take a southern route and meet him in Washington, D.C. He was taking a northern route, carrying a huge wooden cross. We prayed over the phone, and he suggested that we use a Bible as our symbol. That rang a bell with me right away, and I said, "Amen, that's right. The Word of God is where this nation can look for answers."

The seven of us met and decided to push a wheelbarrow full of New Testaments to give to people along the way. We were excited about proclaiming to the nation that God was calling America back to Him. We were all but ready to go when we ran into a battery of opposition.

First, the deacons of a large local church informed us that walking for Christ just wasn't done. They said they had never heard of a group of people selling their belongings to drop out to follow Jesus, except of course in the Bible.

We said, "Praise God, that's right."

Next, several local pastors met with us. They told Ray

that he must not love his wife. The very idea of taking a pregnant woman on a march across the country!

"I don't understand it myself," Ray told them. "I love my wife and I love Jesus. All I can say is that God has called us to go, and we're going."

One of the pastors spoke up. "If God has called these boys, then we'd better not stand in their way."

Then a rumor circulated that we were going to march out of the city with 10,000 young people. The police sent two detectives to investigate me. They went to the local director of the Baptist Student Union and said: "We understand Tippit is trying to get these kids involved in some kind of revolution. Is this true?"

"Yes, sir," he said, "he's trying to get them to have their lives revolutionized by the person of Jesus Christ! He's an activist for the Lord." That satisfied the detectives. They realized that I was not a pied piper.

Arthur called again to be sure I had considered the risk. I thought he was trying to talk me out of going. "Sam, you've got to be 100 percent sure that this is God's will," he said. "Our lives have been threatened, and we may never make it to D.C. You may not either. Pray again and be sure that God is calling you to go."

Before we even could get together for prayer, we met with another obstacle. A young Christian guy came to me and said that he'd had a vision. "God showed me clearly that if you go ahead with this march, you will be struck dead on the first step."

The seven of us—the Monroe 7—got on our knees and prayed that God would lead us. "God, here is the cost. We've lost friends, we may be murdered, and we may even be struck dead on the first step."

While we prayed, Arthur's wife called to ask if we'd

made a decision. We said no, we were still praying. We didn't get back to Arthur until we were under way.

All we had were two cars, a little food, our Bibles, a trailer-tent, and a wheelbarrow. With about $100 between us, and the blessing of God, we planned to leave the next morning, March 16, 1970.

We were too excited to sleep well, but the lack of rest wouldn't take its toll until we were well under way. Dozens of local Christians and several members of the news media gathered to see us off. Many of the kids who had received Christ during the revival joined us in a 7:00 A.M. prayer meeting. I'd made many new friends in Monroe, and I began to wonder if I'd ever see them again. It was an emotional morning.

After we were interviewed briefly by the press, Tex, Ray, Charlotte, Connie, and Little Richard drove ahead in two cars. Ken and I would walk the first leg of the journey. Washington, D.C. was 1,500 miles away. The only definite segment of our schedule was a speaking engagement at Mississippi Baptist College in Jackson. Past that, we just were trusting God to open doors.

As I bent over to grab the wheelbarrow, thoughts raced through my brain. *Will I ever see Leo or Arthur again? Could we be wrong to ignore the death vision? Will we make it to D.C.?* I looked at Ken. "Praise God, brother," I said. "Let's walk for Jesus."

With the first step, my whole being was flooded with the love and the joy of Jesus. God filled my soul and I could only praise Him. I knew we were in His will. Ken and I walked sprightly all morning, reaching the cars in time for the lunch that was brought out by friends from Monroe. We were high on the excitement of being used of God in this unusual way.

Publicity had preceded us, so people knew we were coming. Townspeople gathered, and little kids ran along ahead of us shouting, "Those guys with the wheelbarrow are coming!" It was bright and unusually warm for a March day in Louisiana.

A Black man working in a cornfield in Rayville, Louisiana, was the first to come to Jesus as a result of our walk. We just shared the love of Jesus with him, and he prayed to receive Christ. We witnessed to people all along the way and saw revival in many lives before we finally called it a day.

We set up our tent in the country away from the highway. Ray, Charlotte, Connie, Tex, and I slept in our clothes in the tent while Ken and Richard climbed into their sleeping bags on the ground outside. It had been such a beautiful day.

Then the rain came.

By the time Ken and Richard gathered up their sleeping bags and splashed to the Toyota, they were soaked. They had to sleep sitting up all night. It was still exciting and fun; but when we were greeted in the morning by mud and wet equipment, our spirits were dampened real quicklike. We realized that it wasn't all going to be a high, a joy ride. Already we were down to the nitty-gritty gut level. There wouldn't always be crowds and excitement to keep us going. We needed a special blessing.

Walking twenty-five miles a day, we made it to Jackson, Mississippi, in a week. We stopped at a restaurant just inside the city limits and looked forward to ministering at the college. But we couldn't wait. We started sharing the claims of Jesus right there in the restaurant. Some pastoral students from the college happened to be there, and they didn't appreciate our methods. One preacher boy watched as I talked to a man about his need for forgiveness and salvation. The Holy Spirit dealt with the man's heart, and the man was under conviction. Suddenly he jumped up and stormed out of the place.

"See what you've done," the preacher boy said. "You've turned him off completely. You go around witnessing that way and people will never—"

Just then the man came running back into the restaurant. "Man," he sobbed, "can you come outside and tell me how to get right with God?"

The preacher boys invited us to their room for prayer that night. It turned into an all-night prayer meeting. As we shared our burden to see Christians get right and start winning people to Christ, those students began to confess sin and to pray that God would use them to change the campus.

The next morning we were set to hold an outdoor meeting during the break after the regular campus chapel service. Little Richard was ready to cut loose on his drums, and we just waited for the signal that chapel was over. We figured Little Richard's drum solo would draw the students. We figured right.

Little Richard started banging away. Ray sang a solo, and I preached, and many kids got right with God. Afterward, two local pastors asked us to hold services in their churches. When they heard that we were marching to Washington for Jesus, they took a love offering for us. God was providing.

On our way through Jackson, we took a break and knelt to pray at the side of the road. A car pulled off the road, and a man came to find out what we were all about. He was a minister and thrilled with our mission to call America back to God. He invited us to have a service at his church, and from there we were invited to several other churches and another local college. We saw many come to Christ during four days of ministering in Jackson. We left the next Monday, headed for York, Alabama, and, to our surprise, a chance to witness to Governor George Wallace.

We were trudging through York when we realized that people were hurrying toward the center of the city. We caught wind that Wallace was in town for a rally. Knowing how popular Wallace is in the South and how he is all but worshiped, I was curious to know of his relationship to Christ. We detoured to the rally. We witnessed to many of the hundreds who had gathered, and I asked around to see if I could talk to the governor himself.

I was referred to one of the top dudes. "I'd like to talk to Governor Wallace," I said. "And I'd like to give him one of our Bibles." He said he'd see what he could do. I was just about to resign myself not to see Wallace when the rally started.

A Wallace aide stepped to the microphone to introduce the governor, and another said to me, "We're going to let you do it."

From the platform I heard, "Governor Wallace believes the Bible. He's a real Christian man." They were fixing to use me as a political gimmick.

"Lord," I prayed. "I'm sorry. I didn't come here to be used this way. If I've made a mistake, I'll walk out right now. Lord, tell me what to do." The introductory speech ended, and I was asked to come to the platform to present a Bible to the governor. God impressed these verses on my heart: "And ye shall be brought before governors and kings for my sake. . . . Take no thought how or what you shall speak: for it shall be given you in that same hour what you shall speak. For it is not you that speak, but the Spirit of your Father which speaketh in you" (Matthew 10:18-20).

As I walked toward the platform, I prayed, "OK, Lord, I'm claiming the promise that You'll give me the words." I could hardly believe what came from my mouth.

"People," I began, "the solution to the problems that face our nation today is not found in any politician, but only in the person of Jesus Christ!" I preached Christ for about five minutes and I could see people under conviction and even some crying. The Holy Spirit had taken over.

I turned to the governor. "Governor Wallace, I'd like to give you the Word of God because in it is found the solution to the crises in America." He responded very politely, and I had the impression that he had had no part in the plot to use me for his own gain. So the crowd would know that we were not there for any political reason, we left immediately. Back on the road, we headed for Livingston.

My little presentation had been broadcast over statewide television. Unknown to us, the president of Livingston University had state troopers up and down the highway looking for us all night. He wanted to be sure we didn't pass through Livingston without stopping to speak to the students at the university.

Through speaking at Livingston and on a local radio program, we saw several respond to the claims of Christ. Thrilled and blessed, we kept moving.

As we neared the campus of the University of Alabama at Tuscaloosa a few days later, we passed a chain gang working on the other side of the highway. Holding a big Bible aloft, we yelled across, "Jesus loves you, brothers! Jesus loves you!" A year later I learned that one of the men on that gang met a friend of mine in Baton Rouge, told of seeing us on the highway, and eventually received Christ into his life. Truly, we were used as sowers of the Word.

Officials at the University of Alabama informed us that with all the other Christian organizations holding their clubs and meetings on the campus, they couldn't work us in. They were sorry. We decided that maybe God didn't want us to do anything there in an organized way. We planned just to walk through, witnessing and passing out tracts.

When we got to the student union building there were two longhairs sitting on the front steps. I shared Christ with them. One, looking me in the eye as he strummed his guitar, said: "Man, you've really got something. You should share this with the whole student body."

I told him that the doors had been closed to us. He told us to wait and see if he could do anything. He got permission from the university president for us to hold an outdoor meeting at nine o'clock Monday morning, two weeks to the day since we had left Monroe. We had little time for publicity. We asked God to bless Richard's drums and let them be all the publicity we needed. Those drums had been used in nightclubs for Satan, but Richard turned them over to the Lord. God used them in a mighty way.

When Little Richard cut loose Monday morning, I want to tell you, the kids started coming. I spoke to two thousand that day, and many gave their hearts to Jesus.

As it was during the entire trip, we had nothing definite planned when we strolled into Samford University later in the week. Dr. R. G. Lee, a famous Baptist preacher, was scheduled to speak in chapel, so we went to hear him. Dr. Lee was ill and unable to be there, so it was suggested that the students share testimonies. The first kid who popped up said: "Those guys we read about in the paper are here, the ones with the wheelbarrow full of Bibles. Let's let them tell us what they're doing."

We shared how God had sent revival in Monroe and about our vision for revival in all of America. I also shared the challenge that we were giving Christians—to get right with God and start sharing Christ with a dying nation. God smashed through again.

Students began to confess sin, and many prayed to get right with God. Then another student stood. "I move that we give these guys $100 for more Bibles," he said. The motion passed unanimously and we received a check from their student fund which more than replenished our Bible supply.

We were asked to speak at Hunter Street Baptist Church, one of the largest churches in Birmingham. The service was telecast statewide and brought us invitations from more churches.

There was a carnival going on in a shopping center parking lot in Birmingham, so we invaded that area. We witnessed and passed out tracts when I noticed a teenage nightclub in the shopping center. Tex and Richard and I asked the manager if we could come in. He had read about us in the paper, and he said, "Sure, during intermission you can do your thing."

The combination of drums and preaching was blessed again, and four kids came to know Jesus right there in the nightclub. We left Birmingham knowing that we had not simply come there, but that God had sent us.

We passed out tracts as we walked through Sweetwater, Alabama. The police stopped us at the city limits. They told us it was illegal for us to pass out tracts and that they wouldn't let us walk through their town. We had no room for the wheelbarrow in either of our cars, so we didn't know what to do. A boy we'd been witnessing to turned out to be the nephew of the mayor. "Let's go," he said. "We'll get permission from my uncle."

The city council meeting was just breaking up when we got into town. The police already were there talking to the mayor. As we stood waiting, a city councilman came over. "Are you the boys who are walking to call America back to God?" he asked. "I want you to know that I'm a Christian. I love Jesus and I praise God for what you're doing."

When he heard our problem, he interrupted the policemen. "Mayor, these boys are saying something our country needs to hear. They're saying we should turn our lives over to Jesus Christ."

"All right," the mayor said. "You boys can walk through town." When we got about a mile down the road, the police pulled up. "Hop in the car," one said. *Oh, no,* I thought. The policemen put the wheelbarrow in the trunk. We didn't know what was going on.

They drove out of town and ordered us out of the car at the edge of a woods. I thought of the Monroe boy's vision and of what Arthur had said about the risk. I said: "Sir, we weren't trying to give you any hassle. We just want people to know the Lord. If you don't know Jesus, you can know Him right now—"

"OK," the cop said. "I'm telling you, son, you'd better not ever show your face in this town again. You just start walking and don't let me ever see you again."

I said, "All right, sir, we'll do that. But we want you to know that Jesus loves you and that He died for you. And we love you, too."

As we walked, I prayed, "Lord, You got us through Louisiana, Mississippi, and Alabama, and You've worked in marvelous ways. We don't know exactly what lies ahead, but we know that You're going to do something really great in Georgia." I was right.

On our way to Atlanta, I was contacted by the youth director of churches in the Columbus area. It was time for another God-planned detour. I spoke at a huge rally in Columbus and over thirty kids came to Christ. The news media covered our march and the meeting. We were able to share the claims of Christ on television with the entire city.

The Monroe 7 hadn't had baths since leaving Birmingham. We had been on the road all that time and were pretty grubby. We prayed for a place to sleep. After the rally, the youth director said, "Sam, a lady here offered to let you guys sleep in her big, beautiful home on the riverfront, but I told her y'all would rather sleep in your tent."

"Oh, you didn't tell her that!" I said. "Man, we'd love to stay in her home. We need a bath and a good night's sleep." He caught her, and we took her up on the offer.

While we were in her home that night, Murray Bradfield, another local youth director, came to meet us. I had no idea how important and far-reaching this new acquaintance would be. I never dreamed that two years later Murray and I would be walking for Jesus, carrying a cross across Germany.

Murray invited us to a rally at his church. A speaker had already been lined up, but Murray thought we might just want to get in on it from the listening end for once. The next night, however, God strangely led Ken and Richard and me to a prayer room upstairs rather than into the service.

As the meeting started below, we knelt, crying out to God for revival in America. Psalm 46:10 came to my mind. I said: "Listen, guys, I think God wants us all to hear this.

'Be still, and know that I am God: I will be exalted among the heathen, I will be exalted in the earth.' " We stopped praying aloud. We waited, expecting the presence of God.

In those few quiet moments, God spoke to my heart as He never had before. He said, "I am the God of Abraham, Isaac, and Jacob. I am the Father of many generations who have loved Me. What I have done with Abraham, Isaac, and Jacob, what I have done with Peter and Paul, so will I do with you." I was bubbling over. I shared it with Ken and Richard, and we continued to wait in prayer.

We were almost prostrate on our knees and elbows, hands covering our eyes. Suddenly we broke into uncontrollable sobs. We felt we had been in the presence of Jesus.

I have never felt so unclean, so unworthy. I was broken. When we stopped crying, we again prayed. Each asked God for forgiveness for failing Him so often, and for cleansing and filling, despite our unworthiness. I can't speak for the other guys, but I was filled with peace and joy and power. We were praising God when we finally went downstairs, and everyone down there was praising God. It was a thrilling, enriching day I'm sure none of us will forget.

God chose to meet our needs in that room, so we expected great things in Atlanta. I am convinced that none of what was to happen would have come about had we not waited upon God that evening.

We arrived Friday in the Atlanta suburb of Tucker. I was to speak in three services at the mammoth Rehoboth Baptist Church on Sunday. The pastor told the news media that we were coming; and, after we were interviewed for television, he took us to a radio show. God moved during those thirty minutes, and people called in asking how to be saved. Christians called, wanting to get right with God. On the second most-listened-to station in the state, the show was extended from thirty minutes to one hour and forty-five minutes because the phones wouldn't quit ringing.

On Saturday night we held a youth fellowship service at the church. Several adults showed up also and talked us into going to Underground Atlanta, the big nightclub district beneath the city. We rounded up the laymen and young people from this turned-on church, packed up Little Richard's drums, and prayed, "Lord, touch these drums. Every time Richard beats them, pounce on someone's heart."

Underground Atlanta has everything except auto traffic. Thousands crowded the streets, nightclubs, bars, and shops. The only person doing anything on the street was an organ grinder who had drawn a crowd of less than a hundred. We set up Richard's drums and prayed, "Lord, here goes. We believe You will work in a mighty way."

I had never seen anything like it. Those drums echoed off the underground walls, and people came storming out from everywhere. Establishments emptied in seconds, people streamed onto the street to see what was going on. Even the band came out of one place. I started preaching, and the crowd got so large that we couldn't even see to estimate its number. People couldn't hear in the back, so the church laymen started preaching to little clusters of their own. We blitzed the place with the Gospel of Jesus.

Right in the middle of my preaching, a policeman came up. "I'm sorry," he said, "but you're going to have to quit."

One of the men from the church was a lawyer. He quoted city ordinances until the policeman said, "OK, all right. You can stay."

"I can preach again!" I shouted, and the people roared. I preached against sin, I preached on the power of God, and I preached on the cleansing blood of Jesus. A millionaire banker came up to me and said he'd been thinking about Christ since he heard Billy Graham preach in New York City. He left Underground Atlanta praising God and witnessing.

A lady in the back stood listening with a cocktail glass in her hand. A guy from a nightclub asked her why she didn't come back in and listen to his band. "You're playing for money," she said. "These boys are playing for Jesus. I want to hear what they have to say."

Between church the next morning and the afternoon rally, we had no time to eat. Connie and I were scheduled to be on a television show about drug abuse. In another example of God's timing, the only date this show could get Art Linkletter was the very day we were there. His name drew countless more viewers than normally would watch.

After Connie told how God had released her from the slavery of drugs and how she had fallen in love with Jesus, the moderator turned to me. "How did you get into all this?" he asked.

"Well, I've known people who were into drugs, and—"

"No, no," he interrupted. "I mean your relationship with Christ. How did He come into your life?"

"Praise God," I said, and proceeded to give the entire plan of salvation over statewide television.

A few days later we neared Athens, the home of the University of Georgia. A newsman informed me that the university planned a rally in memory of the students who were killed at Kent State. He said he'd try to get me on the program.

When we arrived, 2,000 students had gathered for the rally. The leader said I could have a couple of minutes to talk. "But," he said, "don't mention the name of Jesus Christ. We also have a rabbi on the platform."

"Well, then count me out," I said. "I won't be on the

program if I can't talk about Jesus. Man, he's what we're all about."

He finally consented; but as it turned out, neither the rabbi nor I were allowed to speak. In the middle of the program, radical students took over the platform. They screamed and shouted, "Let's take over the administration building!" Excited students agreed and followed them to the ad building, abruptly ending the memorial rally.

As I stood watching the kids leave, I could see the steeples of the surrounding community churches and I wondered, *Where are all the Christians?* We were in the Bible Belt. I finally found a guy there from Campus Crusade for Christ. We rounded up a few kids from the Baptist Student Union and stayed up all night, praying and making posters.

Thousands were involved in peace demonstrations the next day, but there also were twenty-five of us Christians marching in and out, passing out Jesus stickers, and wielding posters which said, "Real Peace Is Jesus," and "Get Back to God." One of the signs was held aloft by a bunch of helium balloons.

I worked my way up toward the platform where a radical was shouting obscenities and advocating destruction of city hall. I talked about Jesus to the guys behind him when he suddenly turned and handed me the microphone, thinking I was the next radical in line.

"OK, Lord, here we go again," I prayed.

"There has been a lot of talk here about peace," I began. The crowd cheered. "But let me tell you, there won't be any peace until we get the Prince of Peace, Jesus Christ, into our hearts!" Silence. As I continued to talk about Jesus, I expected a brick or a tomato to come flying, but the students started applauding. The TV cameras came rolling up; and I prayed silently, "Lord, here is a real opportunity to glorify Yourself."

For the next ten minutes I preached Jesus and challenged the students to commit their lives to Him. I often was interrupted by applause. God broke through to those radicals. When I stepped down, I was approached by a national leader of the Students for a Democratic Society. He was big and bad on the outside, but inside he seemed simply to be crying out, "Help me, help me, help me!" I saw God get past the outward toughness and break through to the searching hearts of even the most radical kids.

The next speaker asked, "Well, what *would* Jesus do if He were here?" The riot had turned into a revival. The guy who had told me not to mention the name of Jesus asked me if we would pray that there would be no more violence on the campus. Within an hour after our prayer meeting, the whole demonstration had blown over.

That year, the University of Georgia yearbook carried a picture of Tex and Connie holding a big sign, "Real Peace Is Jesus."

4 / Hassles, Lessons, and God's Power

As we walked from Georgia to South Carolina, our eyes really were turned toward Washington, D.C. It seemed as if we were almost there. Our destination soon would become a reality. The last leg of the journey, however, was the toughest. God had several lessons to teach us before we were through. The first lesson was wisdom.

The first place we camped out in South Carolina was filled with scorpions. We had to put the girls in a hotel for the night and admit that we should have scouted our campsite more thoroughly.

Another lesson we learned as we neared Washington was love for our enemies. Often while we were walking, truck drivers whizzed close to us on the shoulder at about sixty mph and then pulled back onto the highway, just to scare us. We never worried much about it, but we didn't like it. One day, as Ken and I were walking, we heard a huge trailer truck roar up behind us. The driver pointed his finger at us, pulled onto the shoulder, and barreled straight for us. At the last instant we realized it was no game.

We took one quick step and hurled ourselves off the shoulder and into the ditch, wheelbarrow, Bibles, and all. The truck missed us by inches and narrowly missed tumbling into the ditch itself. We knelt right there and prayed for that truck driver. "Somehow help us to love him. We know he needs You, and we pray that You'll break his heart for You."

Tex's younger brother, Mike Sirman, joined us on the march in the Carolinas. He and I were walking when we met the next crisis. People often pulled off the road to ask us what we were doing, and we always took the opportunity to share Christ. But one man who pulled off seemed almost possessed.

He screamed at us, yelled that he should kill us, and threatened to beat us up. He shouted obscenities and kept ranting, but God gave me a supernatural love for him. As he carried on, I looked him in the eye and said, "Sir, I love you."

"I don't care!" he screeched. "You should be dead, and I ought to be the one to kill you!"

"Mike," I said, "let's pray." We dropped to our knees right in front of him and prayed that God would get hold of him and show him that we loved him. The guy was flabbergasted. He said nothing while we prayed. He stood in the road and was almost hit a couple of times. We just stayed on our knees. Finally he jumped in his car and sped off.

Another time, Richard and I learned the value of God's supernatural protection. We paid little attention to the traffic on the highway until one car slowed as it came by. A pistol appeared from the passenger's side and a shot rang out. We didn't even have time to duck. If a bullet actually was fired, God redirected it, because there was little chance that it could have missed at that range.

One of the freakiest encounters we had on the march was with two German shepherds. They were kept in a high-fenced pen just off the highway. As Richard and I walked by, their owner came out, opened the gate, pointed at us, and shouted, "Get 'em!"

Those huge dogs came bounding at us, snorting and growling. We froze. I thought I was about to die. "Lord, what do I do now?" I prayed. I pointed at the dogs and shouted at the top of my lungs, "*I command you in the name of Jesus Christ to go back!*" The dogs skidded to a stop, turned around, and scampered back. The owner scratched his head.

He pointed at us again. "I said to get 'em!" he said. The dogs came charging at us again.

Louder even than before, I shouted, "*In the name of Jesus Christ, I command you to go back!*" Again the dogs stopped and trotted back. The guy locked them in the pen and walked to his house, shaking his head. We kept walking for Jesus, our legs a little rubbery.

Probably the greatest lesson God taught us was love for each other. It's easy to show love to someone you really don't know. But Jesus said that men shall know we are His disciples if we love one another. That was tough on the road. Sleeping was a hassle because we had to sleep in our clothes. We were dirty and hot and tired and miserable. We started to complain once, and that was when God quit blessing; not before we started complaining, but *because* we complained.

God miraculously provided money and food all along the way. We were down to just some Kool-Aid, peanut butter, and bread. At the end of the day, when all you've had to eat was a scoop of grits, you need more than half of a peanut butter sandwich and half a glass of Kool-Aid for supper. Selfish attitudes started to emerge.

I remember one miserable, sticky day when I sat down with my sandwich and a swallow or two of Kool-Aid and noticed another half glass or so in the pitcher. I started thinking, *I'll bet ol' Ray wants that Kool-Aid and I'm not going to get it*. It sounds ridiculous, but at the time it seemed so important. We got irritated with each other, and consequently our supplies ran out. God had to teach us really to die to self daily.

One morning I woke up with the blahs. I felt terrible. I didn't want to go back out on the road, but I knew I had to. I didn't want to walk. I didn't want to witness. And I didn't want to love. What I felt like doing was staying in bed.

All the other guys were up and busy, so I felt obligated. This was the only day I walked out of a feeling of obligation rather than of dedication. I didn't even care, but I *did* care that I didn't care. I prayed: "Lord, make me care. I can't do it. I feel awful, but I know You want me to witness, so work in me."

The first two guys I met were truck drivers who had pulled onto the shoulder for coffee. I felt nothing for them, but I knew that God wanted me to witness to them. As I told them about Jesus, God filled my heart with love. I really began to feel for their souls. Though they didn't receive Christ, I know that they were there for a purpose. God showed me that, if I will just step out in faith and obedience, He will add the feeling. He cares more about souls than I ever could.

Later in the day we stopped at a gas station where we saw two young men. "Hi, guys," I said. "Jesus loves you."

"Right," one replied, obviously drunk. "You want some booze?"

"No. Jesus set me free from booze."

"Who do you guys think you are with this wheelbarrow?"

"We don't think we're anybody," I said. "But we have

Somebody living inside us that we think is very important. We will do anything to bring this country back to God."

Slowly their attitudes changed, and they began to ask questions. They asked how we had come to know Christ. I shared some Scripture and told them how God had changed my life. "Look, if you want to know Jesus, you can pray with us right now." They did. We had reacted to their hatred with love, and that had made the difference. That was a great lesson for me. Love conquers all.

The day finally came when we were to walk across the bridge over the Potomac River into Washington, D.C. As we started across, we praised God for the past four months and 1,500 miles. We'd had some rough times, some good times, many great times, but most of all, blessed times with Jesus. But our walk wasn't finished yet. Crossing the bridge was an experience in itself.

Three Black guys stopped us as we neared the city. They shouted Black power slogans. One guy pulled me off to the side. "I'll kill you," he said.

As he reared back to slug me, I said, "Jesus loves you." His hand stopped. He pulled it back again. "Jesus loves you," I said. He stopped again. Something held him back. The love of Jesus.

"Man, I hate you!" he snarled. "You whites have been putting my people down for so long."

"But Jesus loves you," I said. "Maybe some whites are putting you down, but I love you, brother."

He pulled his fist back again. "Don't you tell me that, whitey!"

"Jesus loves you," I said again and again. He kept cocking his arm, but never swung.

"How can you love me? How can Jesus love me? Is Jesus white?"

"I don't know, man. I've never seen Him. Those that worship Him must worship Him in spirit and truth, the Bible says. Before I came to Christ, I hated Black people. I had prejudice in my heart and I thought Black people were lower than whites. [His arm was still raised to strike me.] But, man, when Jesus took over my life, He took away that prejudice and filled me with love. That's why I can stand here right now and say from the bottom of my heart that I love you."

"You mean that?"

"Yes, I sure do."

"Honest?"

"Honest. I'm not just talking. I love you and I want you to know my Jesus."

He stuck out his hand. "Man," he said. "You're OK."

"No. Jesus is OK. I'm rotten. If it was up to me, I would probably still be a hater. Jesus changed me." We wound up kneeling together for prayer. Though he didn't receive Christ, the love of Jesus had started to work in his life. And I had learned another lesson in love.

It was great to see Arthur again. After we shared experiences from our walks, he filled me in on the plans for the next few days. Rallies were scheduled every night for the next three days at Capitol Hill Metropolitan Baptist Church, and then hundreds of Christians would march across the city.

During the day, local kids joined Arthur and our group in street witnessing. One day Tex and I found ourselves in the Capitol building in a restricted corridor where the senators came out of their chambers. I still don't know how we got there. We got a chance to share with several legislators our hope for the nation: Jesus Christ.

Murray Bradfield, who had met us there, and another

friend and I decided to do a little witnessing by car one day. When we came to a red light, we'd all jump out and pass out tracts and witness, trying to get back to the car in time for the green light. We were having fun and sharing Christ at the same time.

I started witnessing to a man and didn't get back in the car in time. The traffic in Washington is terrible. The way the streets are set up, it would be quite a while before the car could get back to where they'd left me. I was totally disoriented. "Lord," I prayed, "You've got a reason for this, so I'm trusting You to lead me wherever I'm supposed to go."

I walked fast, passing out Jesus stickers and tracts, witnessing as I went. After several minutes I came to a gate and a big, black iron fence. I looked between the bars, and there was the White House. "Thank You, Lord." I thought maybe He would give me a chance to witness to Princess Grace, who happened to be visiting that day. I realized that thousands of people look through this fence daily to see who they can see. So, I started pasting stickers on the fence about every fourth bar. People gathered around the bars to read, "Real Peace Is Jesus."

I went by the guard at the gate and started on the other end of the fence. I had covered the entire first end when two guards came running out. "Hey, you!" they yelled. "Come here!" They pulled out a knife. "You see this?" they asked.

"Y-yes, sir," I said.

"You're going to take this and scrape off all those stickers, or we'll arrest you for defacing government property!"

"Yes, sir," I said. "I'll do it right now. Forgive me. I had no idea it was against the law."

The guard followed me around to make sure I'd do it,

and I got a good chance to witness to him. I scraped all the stickers from one end and he asked, "Is that all?"

I said, "No. There are some on the other end too."

"Well," he said, "I'll trust you to scrape them off. You're a good Christian."

When I brought the knife back to him, he told me that I could pass out literature but that I couldn't paste on any more stickers. So I went back just to passing out tracts.

"Halt!" The gate opened automatically and a guard called me in.

What have I done now? I thought.

He took me into a little office and pawed a radio handset from the wall. "I've got him here," he said. "He's under guard. Send someone to pick him up."

"Lord, I'm sorry," I prayed. "I didn't know I was doing anything wrong."

A guard came over and said, "Follow me." As we walked toward the White House, he said, "What were you doing anyway?"

When I told him, he said: "Then you're a Christian! Praise the Lord! I am, too! That's great. We need more young people doing this."

He took me to the top security man's office and showed me the pictures the secret service had taken of me sticking stickers and passing out tracts. They took my driver's license and ran an FBI check on me. While I waited, the Christian guard kept sicing me onto the people who were coming through to get press credentials. "There's a television man with a filthy mouth," he'd say. Or, "There's a guy who really needs Christ." I witnessed to lots of people in there.

The top security officer came in and said, "Tippit, if we can get you on something, we will."

"Sir, I'm sorry. I really apologize. I didn't know I was doing anything wrong." Then I started thinking. *If this guy is in charge of security, he has access to the princess.* "Sir, could you do me a favor? Could you have one of your men give the princess one of these tracts?"

"What!? Don't you say anything about the princess around here. You're not going to get near her!"

When my record came back clean, the top dude said, "We're releasing you, and you can hand out tracts; but don't stop and talk to anyone. Understand?"

"Yes, sir," I promised. They watched me as I walked away. I handed a tract to two Black girls and kept walking. They came running back. *Oh, no,* I thought.

"Hey, man, listen," one said. "We've been thinking about this. I've been laying awake nights worrying about whether or not I'm going to heaven. Do you know how I can have that assurance?"

I talked without looking back. "Do you want to know Jesus?"

"Yes."

We knelt right on the sidewalk and prayed, and they received Christ. I kept expecting someone to shout "Halt!" but no one hassled us. I got up and kept walking and never looked back. Truly God had sent me to the White House.

July 17, 1970, finally came. We were to have a big rally at the Washington Monument after marching to the Capitol and back. People flooded the area for the rally. We were proclaiming to the nation's leaders that Jesus is the only hope. The rally culminated a twenty-four-hour prayer vigil.

About a thousand gathered, and God blessed all of us who testified. The Spirit laid it upon Arthur's heart to fast for forty days at the corner of Constitution Avenue and

15th Avenue, praying for revival in America. I decided to spend a little time with him there. I'll never forget pushing that wheelbarrow with Arthur as he carried a cross to the corner where he was to spend the next six weeks of his life.

Arthur usually had quite a crowd around him at the corner during the day, but at night, things were pretty quiet. As he dozed in the wee hours one morning, I prayed that God would use me that very day to spark revival in America. The pay phone at the corner rang. Arthur had released the number to the local press.

The caller was a disc jockey from Boston. "I've heard about what you guys are doing," he said. "I'd just like a little more information."

"Are you a Christian?" I asked.

"No. I'm Jewish."

"Praise God," I said. "Jesus was Jewish." I went through the entire plan of salvation then led him in a little prayer of acceptance. After we prayed, he asked me to repeat the telephone number. I told him we'd send him some follow-up material so he could grow in the Lord. We talked for several minutes, and I was thrilled to be able to tell him about Christ. I thanked God.

A few minutes later the phone rang again. It was a girl from Pennsylvania. *Wow*, I thought, *this number has really gotten around!*

"I praise God for what you guys are doing," she said.

"What do you mean?" I asked.

"Well, I just heard you on the radio, and—"

"On the radio? No, you didn't hear me on the—"

"Weren't you just on the radio?"

"No."

"Didn't you just pray with a guy from Boston?"

"Yes. How did you know that?"

"You were live on the radio, man!" She promised to pray with us for revival in America.

Seconds after I hung up, the phone rang again. It was a man from North Carolina. "I'm going to wake up my pastor right now," he said. "We're going to pray with you for revival."

The next call was from a truck driver. He was crying. "I heard you on the radio as I was driving through the mountains," he managed. "I've been searching for two years. How can I know God?" Praise the Lord, I led him to Christ over the phone.

I found out the next day that the disc jockey really had not received Christ but had repeated the prayer so his listeners could hear it. God had used this Jew as an instrument to get His message to much of the nation. The show was broadcast over a wide area. God had answered my prayer in a surprising and unique way.

5 / God's Love in Action

Roger McKin was huge. We called him the Bear. Bear received Christ at a rally in Tulsa where I had given my testimony. Jesus saved him from a life of crime, and he really was a new creature. Despite a history of doing dope, knifing, stealing, and even serving a hitch at Leavenworth Prison, Bear was a new man for sure. He wouldn't hurt a flea.

God had been impressing upon my heart that I should set up a headquarters and start a street ministry in Chicago. So, after a week with Arthur, Tex and I headed for Baton Rouge to spend a few days with my mother and make plans for Chicago. It was a sad day when we left our friends in Washington, but many great things lay ahead. I decided that our evangelistic outreach should minister under the label, "God's Love in Action," for the Lord had taught me love *and* action in the past several months. I looked forward to some rest and then a real fruitful ministry in the Windy City.

Bear was the only one with us when Tex and I arrived in Chicago on September 1, 1970. Chicago lowered him to a scaredy-cat. He was afraid even to sleep alone. He always wanted to drag his bed into our room at night. "Sam," he said, "I know what kinda people there are here; and, now

66

that I'm a Christian, I'd have to turn the other cheek instead of smashing them. Let me sleep in your room."

We were praying in a church one night with the lights off when Bear heard water dripping. It was coming from the baptismal tank. "Sam, do you think that's the devil?" he asked.

"No, it's just water dripping."

It kept getting louder. Drip, drip, drip. "I'm sure that's the devil, Sam!"

"No, Bear, it's not the devil."

Then we heard footsteps coming down the aisle. Bear jumped to his feet and shouted, "Devil, I command you in the name of Jesus to get out of here!" The lights went on, and it was the pastor! We cracked up.

We lived with some Moody Bible Institute students in a big house in Uptown, Chicago's North Side ghetto. It was a real bad neighborhood. When the Moody kids left for school in the fall, we were left renting the upstairs for $200 a month. With no steady source of income, and only the knowledge that God wanted us to start a work in Chicago, we trusted Him to provide. He always did.

The first time we went out witnessing, we were surprised. Street witnessing just was not done in Chicago on any regular basis. Some Moody kids were involved on weekends with the Open Air Campaigners who frequently hit Old Town and the ghetto areas with a van and mini-meetings, but one-to-one type witnessing was rare.

The response was discouraging. People didn't trust us. We saw a rat that first night, and we walked around scatterings of glass in our bare feet. "Why doesn't your Jesus get you some shoes?" a girl asked. Only then did we realize that Northerners don't run around city streets without shoes.

For the first time in my ministry I saw no results. None. I had been spoiled by seeing God work in mighty ways in the South and in Washington, D.C. Now it was time for a real lesson in patience and persistence.

Our expenses neared $400 each month, and God always gave us just enough. Our support came almost exclusively from individuals, and never the same ones. A couple of Sunday school classes sent us about $15 a month each. We never have asked for a penny. We always are happy to share our mission and put someone on our newsletter mailing list, but we are a faith ministry and trust God to supply our needs.

I knew we were in God's will because He kept supplying our physical needs, but the lack of fruit was getting to me. We prayed constantly that the Spirit of God would move on the city and that souls would be saved. If I'd ever had a problem with pride before, it was cured in Chicago when I saw without doubt that no one comes to Christ unless the Holy Spirit of God works in his life.

Finally, after three months of barrenness, Big Mike came to Jesus. Mike Logston was a professional thief from Oklahoma who came to Chicago because, he said, the thieving was easier. This six foot four inch, 280 pounder always carried a sawed-off shotgun. He ran into the Bear one night in Old Town, and the next day he was a babe in Christ. It was a real thrill, a major breakthrough. God had saved another big, tough, bad man like Bear.

Within twenty-four hours, a Jewish girl, Cindy, gave her heart to Jesus. She was a runaway who ran smack into the Lord. After that, God really began to bless. We decided to start Bible study classes at our place on Monday nights. The first Monday night, Tex and I were the only ones there.

Neither of our two new converts could make it, and Bear had been called home.

His wife, who had left him a year or so before, got right with Jesus and called him. We were happy for him and praised God that his marriage was salvaged, but there we were, alone against the city, with no choice but to turn to God for everything.

Tex and I kept witnessing on the streets and invited interested kids to our Monday evening studies. We held them every Monday, regardless of how many people showed up. Soon we filled our attic with kids each week.

I received more and more invitations to preach at churches around the Midwest, and these speaking engagements helped to pay most of our bills. We never worried that God would provide a little more when the time came that we had another mouth to feed. In fact, we started keeping our eyes open for more staff members.

I met Lloyd Cole, an associate pastor, when I preached at a church in Bluefield, West Virginia. We had a great time of revival down there, and Lloyd seemed like a great guy, but I sensed that something was missing.

A few days after I returned to Chicago, I received a long-distance call at six o'clock in the morning. It was Lloyd.

"Sam," he said, "I'm not a Christian."

"What do you mean?" I slurred, rubbing my eyes.

"I've never opened my heart to Jesus."

"The devil is trying to make you doubt, Lloyd," I said. "We all go through that. You're a Christian."

"Listen, Sam, when I was a boy I walked down the aisle and made a profession of faith because I felt my parents wanted me to. After that there was always an emptiness, and people said what I needed was to teach a Sunday school class. Then they said what I needed was to be a youth director. After that they said I felt empty because I needed to preach. Now I've done everything, and I'm still miserable. I have no relationship with Christ."

"Lloyd, let's pray." He came to know Christ right there on the phone. About three weeks later he joined our staff as my associate. He brought with him a young man from Marengo, Illinois, named Dwight Wirsing, who planned to start at Moody in the fall. Ricky Auxier and Gordy Harbeck, two Chicago area boys, also joined us, so we had four other full-timers when the Bible studies really started to click.

The big daily papers in Chicago considered us the originators of the Jesus Movement in Chicago. We often were referred to as Jesus Freaks or Jesus People.

There were parts of the movement which we definitely did not want to be associated with, but we never said so publicly. We were too busy to hassle phonies. There was a kind of a "Jesus-ology" in some segments of the movement. We were not into the Superstar business at all. To me, Jesus is the Son of God, the Christ, the Messiah, the Lord of lords, the King of kings.

On the other end of the spectrum was a bunch of fundamentalists like us, but who were into the fad thing. They wore Jesus Christ watches, Jesus T-shirts, and even Jesus jockey shorts. They figured, "Man, if you're a freaky Christian, that's where it's at." Much of the Jesus Movement was of God, but I'm afraid many kids were just into the fad end of it. Because we were young, the news media often identified us with the movement. We'd been called worse names, but we really were old-fashioned Christians.

Within half a year our Bible studies averaged sixty kids each week. Two months later, in July of 1971, we had 600 kids in four weeks. All we did was study, sing, and pray, but the new Christians were hungry to learn about Jesus.

I preached in a church one Sunday on Abraham and how he had stepped out on faith. As I told how God had promised him a son, I had trouble keeping my train of thought. God was trying to tell me something. As I preached on the idea of trusting God in the spirit of Abraham, God told me that I would have a son and that my son would be used of God in a mighty way.

I didn't necessarily prefer a son, but there was no doubt in my mind that God had promised me one. Tex was skeptical. "I believe it could happen because I've seen the Lord do so many things," she said, "but what if we had a girl?" We didn't know it, but she already was pregnant.

When we found out, we prayed about a name. No names for girls even entered our minds. Tex began to be convinced. All we could think of was Paul David. Besides the fact that my father's name was David, I was always intrigued with the David of the Bible. And I believe that Paul was one of the greatest men who ever lived. I wanted my son to exemplify Galatians 2:20 and Philippians 1:21.

As I kept praying about the matter, I became more and more convinced that God was going to give us a son. Finally, in a city-wide crusade in East St. Louis, Illinois, I spilled the beans. I stood before 2,000 people and announced that God had promised us a son. People came to me later and said, "What if it's a girl?"

"It's not going to be a girl." I smiled. Even Tex was convinced by this time, but I'm not sure she was excited about my announcing it.

During the summer, Arthur came to Chicago, and we held a giant rally in the Civic Center Plaza. More than a thousand people gathered, and many threw away dope and booze and turned their lives over to Jesus. Our Bible studies grew, and we saw more and more results on the street.

The famous acid rock music group, "Sly and the Family Stone," played for about ten thousand kids at a festival at Northwestern University in Evanston, north of Chicago. We went to share Jesus. It really was wild. Kids lay naked on the beach, and drugs were passed around openly. I could hardly believe my eyes.

We passed out little red stickers which had our name and address and "One Way, Trust Jesus," written on them. We called them "reds," the word for downers in the drug scene. Ricky stood in the middle of the crowd of hippies and yelled, "Free reds right here! All you want!" Kids flocked around him. Some were disappointed. Some weren't.

I met one girl who was stoned on Orange Sunshine, a concentrated form of LSD that really had her high. I prayed for her, and God brought her down. Then she prayed to receive Him. It was a miracle.

Back at headquarters we painted "Jesus Loves You" on one of our upstairs windows. A girl saw it and stopped to see me. "I ran away from home in Washington, D.C.," she began. "I thought I could really find out what was happening if I came to Chicago.

"I've already been raped," she sobbed. "I'm into drugs and I'm strung out. I was walking down the street and I saw your sign. Jesus touched me."

I asked her if she wanted to give her heart to Jesus and get her sins forgiven and her life changed. She did, so we prayed. Then we called her parents in D.C., arranged for her to get home, and even contacted some good Christians there so she could have fellowship. God had led her down our street. Some may think we were religious fanatics to have "Jesus Loves You" painted in bright colors on our window, but one girl is glad we did.

We sought out an occasion to share Christ with the Satan worshipers in Chicago. Tex and I stopped in their coffeehouse to talk to one of the leaders. After we talked for a while, he said, "Tippit, I have more power in my little finger than all the Christians in Chicago."

I said, "I challenge you on that."

That bothered him a little. "What do you mean?"

"I challenge you. Prove it."

He didn't know what to say.

When Tex and I left him, we walked up and down the street praying that God would remove the power of Satan from the streets. The next night there was no Satan literature being distributed, and the leader was not to be found. One month later, that coffeehouse burned to the ground. Praise God, we worship the victorious Christ.

6 / Hauled Before Magistrates

In the nightclub district, centered around Rush Street, we met many people who weren't true nightclubbers. They were lonely people—people who would walk the streets and go into a club just to find something, any kind of peace or love or happiness.

The nightclub owners didn't appreciate our coming around. One night I got a phone call from an owner who refused to give his name. "I don't want to see you down here anymore," he said.

"Well, sir," I said, "we're not doing anything but talking to people, and only if they want to talk. We're not going inside your club. We're staying on the sidewalk."

"Well, I'm telling you that I don't want you down here. People don't want to hear about your religion, and you're hurting our business. People come down here to have a good time, so you stay away."

"Sir, I'm not trying to be obnoxious, but God has told us to go where the people are. I respect your opinion, but there are people down there that need the ministry God has given us."

"All right," he said, "you come down here, but I'm telling you I'll have you thrown in jail."

"All right. Jesus loves you."

Our most serious hassle came from "My Place," a club

74

just off Rush Street on Delaware Street. Arthur Blessitt's ministry for Jesus on the Sunset Strip was called "His Place"; the coffeehouse ministry for Jesus in Monroe, Louisiana, was called "Your Place"; now we are encountering an ungodly establishment, appropriately called "My Place."

The "My Place" doorman, LeRoy, tried to put the heat on Lloyd Cole one night. He wasn't a big guy, but he told Lloyd that he had rumbled with gangs in Chicago and was used to knifing people. "And I wouldn't mind cutting up you guys if you keep coming down here," he warned.

Lloyd explained to him that we weren't there to hurt business but to share the claims of Christ with anyone who'd listen. "If it happens that this hurts business, that's too bad," Lloyd said. "We don't have anything against anyone. We just want to share the love of Jesus." Many of the clubs began closing down at midnight instead of four o'clock in the morning as usual.

On September 1, 1971, I returned to Chicago from a week of meetings in Florida. Tex and Lloyd met me at the plane. It was a year to the day since Tex and I first arrived in Chicago to set up our ministry. Tex was eight months pregnant, and I was excited to see her. But I could tell immediately that something was wrong. "What's up?" I asked.

"Sam," Lloyd said, "Danny and Paul have been arrested."

"Arrested? For what?"

"For witnessing."

Danny and Paul weren't obnoxious types. They really had a burden and compassion for souls. "Lloyd," I said, "what happened?"

Danny and Paul, high school seniors, were dynamic, witnessing Christians at school and on the street. They had

joined us often during the summer and were two of the
most mature high schoolers I'd ever worked with. Paul
(we called him M because his last name was Mungredies)
was a transfer student from Turkey. A conviction would
jeopardize his visa.

"The nightclub owners carried out their threats," Lloyd
said. Lloyd and the boys had split up and were witnessing
on Delaware Street. Lloyd was into a pretty heavy rap
with a guy, when he saw Danny and M being hustled into a
paddy wagon. They had handed a tract to a man when
two plainclothesmen flipped a badge on them and arrested
them.

Lloyd wasn't allowed to ride in the squad car, so he followed them to the police station, then picked up Tex and
came to get me. By the time we got home, it was after
midnight. After they were bailed out, M went to his home,
but Danny came back to the house with me. I quizzed him,
trying to find out exactly what had happened.

"Did you provoke anyone? Have any hassles?"

He told me that they simply had been arrested right away
and charged with disorderly conduct. I could hardly believe it. Danny and I got on our knees and poured out our
hearts to God. I was in constant prayer about it all during
the next day. My heart was broken that our ministry could
be jeopardized by two boys getting arrested for witnessing.
It didn't make sense.

Friday night, September 3, Lloyd and I went down to
witness on Delaware Street. We weren't asking for trouble.
This was our mission field, and we would not be intimi-
dated. The very same thing took place.

The first person I handed a tract to was a plainclothesman. "I'm sorry," he said, "but you aren't going to be able
to do this here tonight. It's not legal."

"What's wrong with it?"

"You're just going to have to take my word for it. Now I'm telling you that you can't do this here."

"Sir, if we're doing something wrong, we'll leave. Really, we will. I believe in obeying the law; so please, tell us, what are we doing wrong?"

"I'm telling you, you'll have to leave!"

"What are we doing wrong? If this is illegal and I'm infringing on someone else's rights, I'll leave."

He pulled me off to the side. "Listen, I'll tell you what you're doing wrong. You're taking food out of a baby's mouth."

"What?"

"The man who owns this place supports his family by providing entertainment and selling booze. You're hurting his business. Do you think it's right to deprive a man of his job?"

"I believe that if the man seeks God's will in his life, God will provide him with a better job than he has now. He won't have to live in sin. If we have revival in America, a lot of nightclub owners will be out of work."

"Well, you're hurting this man and his business and a lot of other people down here."

"That's your opinion," I said. "There are pushers and prostitutes walking these streets. Certainly we aren't doing anything illegal like they are. We're offering something positive, and they are ruining people's lives. We're just sharing Christ with lonely people. If we're doing something wrong, I'll be more than happy to leave. But if we're not, I'm going to stay."

"Listen," he said, "why don't you go downtown and do it?"

"If it's wrong here, it would be just as wrong down there, wouldn't it?"

"Don't worry," he said. "If you don't leave, we'll get something on you."

I was assured of God that we were doing the right thing when the next person I talked to received Christ after about a half hour of rapping. He knelt right there on the sidewalk and prayed with me. Then I noticed LeRoy, the doorman. He came out of "My Place" and pulled a knife from his pocket.

The man I was talking to didn't notice, and after he left, I felt I should get with Lloyd who was at the other end of the street, past the nightclub. As I walked past the club, as close to the street as I could, LeRoy came toward me with his knife. He flipped his wrist to make the four-to-five-inch blade snap. I quickened my pace, praying silently that God would take over the situation. LeRoy got within a few feet of me, and I started to jog. I felt sure he was about to knife me; I decided that if he did, I would just fall to my knees and pray. I wasn't prepared physically to defend myself against a knife.

As I got several feet from the nightclub entrance, LeRoy stopped his pursuit. Lloyd and I talked with two older people about Christ for awhile, and I kept my eye on LeRoy. Then the two plainclothesmen came out of the nightclub and walked past us. *They're policemen,* I reasoned, *I should tell them about LeRoy.*

"Sirs, could I talk with you a minute?"

"We have nothing to talk to you about. You're the one who's doing everything right, remember?"

"But someone pulled a weapon on me."

"A weapon? Where? What did it look like?" The policeman was talking loudly so LeRoy could hear. When I pointed at LeRoy, the policeman moved toward him, and LeRoy ran into the alley next to the club. Instead of searching him or looking in the alley for a knife, the policeman brought LeRoy to the front of the club and searched him. "There's no knife on him!" the policeman said. "Are you trying to cause trouble?"

"Did you check the alley?" I asked. "If he wants to throw the knife away, that's fine with me. I just want to be able to witness for Jesus without being hassled or worrying about getting knifed."

"You're here to cause trouble!"

"No, sir, we're not. We feel that *our* rights have been infringed upon. We just want to freely witness for Christ. The law has been broken against us." I couldn't back down now.

"You've got five minutes to get off these streets!"

"Wait a minute. Why? You haven't told me what we are doing wrong!"

"You want a law? I'll give you a law. Loitering."

"We can't get them on that," the other policeman said. "They're not loitering."

They argued among themselves about what they'd get us for. One said "disorderly conduct," and the other said "littering."

"No," the first said, "there are no tracts on the street. But don't worry, son, we'll get you on something."

"But you haven't told me what we're—"

"All right, you're under arrest."

"Sir, we don't have to go through all this."

"Just shut up. I don't want to hear any more."

When a squad car pulled up to take us to the police station, the policeman called Lloyd over. "That's right," he said. "Both of you." We had a good rap with the uniformed officers in the car. They couldn't understand why we'd been busted.

We got to the station near the corner of Chicago Avenue and LaSalle Street a little after 10:00 P.M. As the desk officer filled out a report on us, we were searched and our Bibles and literature were taken. "Why don't you let the boys keep their Bibles and tracts?" I couldn't believe it. It was the plainclothesman! "It won't hurt anything for them just to read."

I was really confused. His whole attitude had changed. "Sir," I said, "do you know that Jesus really loves you?"

"Yeah, yeah," he said, "I know. For God so loved the world, and all that."

"Do you know the Bible?"

"Sure. I know all about the Bible!"

"Do you know Jesus?"

"Well, I wouldn't exactly call myself a Christian."

"Jesus could come into your heart."

"I know. I know. You fellas go ahead and make your phone call."

I called Tex. She almost cried. We would have to wait in a cell until someone from the house came with bail.

Despite the attempt by the arresting officer, we were not allowed to take our Bibles and tracts into the cell. We were led down a gray corridor with cells on either side. The noise and the stench were terrible. In the first cell were several drunks, many of whom just slept on the floor. In the other cells, Blacks and whites separated, prisoners yelled at each other.

Lloyd and I were put in an empty cell at one end. The other prisoners were out of our view. In our cell was a toilet and sink combination and two steel slabs which jutted out from the wall for beds. The door clanged shut.

Lloyd and I sat down on one of the steel slabs and just looked at each other. "I can't believe it, man," I said. "Before I got saved I never went to jail. Here I am, saved and in jail. All the testimonies I've ever heard went the other way." Neither of us laughed.

"What're we gonna do, Sam?"

"Let's pray."

As we prayed, God filled our hearts with peace. We were reminded of Philippians 4:6-7, "Be careful for nothing; but in every thing by prayer and supplication with thanksgiving let your requests be made known unto God. And the peace of God, which passeth all understanding, shall keep your hearts and minds through Christ Jesus."

"Lloyd," I said, "there are people in here who need Jesus Christ."

First we sang. Then we shouted our testimonies. Things were quiet for a few seconds; but, when the prisoners heard what we were doing, they banged on the bars and shouted for us to shut up. "We don't want to hear that!" they yelled.

We testified to the power of God to change lives. The men would get noisy and then quiet and then get noisy again. After about fifteen minutes of sticking with it, we noticed that the noise had all but subsided. From the other end of the cell block, a voice called out, "Hey, are you a preacher?"

"Yes, sir, I am."

"What're you doing in jail?"

I told him how we'd been busted, and that seemed to give us a common ground. A Black man in the cell right next to us said, "You talk about having peace in your heart. Man, I've been searchin' for peace for six years. How do you get that peace?"

I couldn't see him, but I knew he was just inches away,

listening as I talked about Jesus. "Lloyd, I wish we had a tract to give him." Lloyd fished in his back pocket and beamed.

"Here's one they didn't find," he said. Lloyd twisted his arm out through the bar and tried to hand the tract to the man. Just as the Black man reached for it, the tract slipped from Lloyd's fingers and floated to the floor. He quickly grabbed his comb, stabbed at the tract, and carefully slid it as far as he could toward the other cell. The man snatched it up.

The whole place was quiet as we waited for the man's reaction. After several minutes, I asked, "What's happening, brother?"

"This says a lot," he said in just over a whisper. "I want to know God."

"Are you willing to pray with us right here?"

"Yes."

"Even aloud in front of all these guys?"

"Yes."

We prayed for him, and then he prayed. He admitted that he was a sinner, and he thanked Jesus for dying for him. Then he invited Christ into his life. We told him that, when he got out of jail, he should look us up so we could help him. "I'm gonna be here for a long time," he said. "I cut up a dude and they found the knife on me." But Jesus had saved him. Lloyd was bubbling over. He told me it was near midnight. We thought of Paul and Silas in jail and how a man had come to Christ at midnight.

"Sammy, let's lead these guys in singing with us."

"This isn't a church crowd, Lloyd. You're not going to get them to sing. These are bad dudes."

"Wait a minute," he said. "Let me try. You all know

'Amazing Grace'? [It was high on the pop charts at the time.] We'll sing and you follow!"

We started singing; and, sure enough, the men knew the song. It was an indescribable thrill. Here were these criminals, none of them real singers, growling and mumbling along, off-key and sour, but enjoying singing "Amazing Grace." It was a sweet, discordant sound. When we finished, I preached on Acts 16 and told the men how they could have peace with God even in jail.

When Dwight Wirsing came with the bond money, we left, grateful for the opportunity to hold a revival at the midnight hour but worried about our ministry. M was waiting for us when we got to the house.

"Sam, what are we going to do? This is four busts in three days. We haven't got the bread for any more bail."

Tex came in and threw her arms around me. "Are you all right?" she asked.

"Sure, baby." I told her all that had happened and that I wanted to stay up to pray alone. M asked if he could pray with me.

As we prayed, I began to realize how far-reaching these arrests could be. Not only were we being denied our right to freedom of speech, but all the other ministries whose work depended on street witnessing were in trouble. I thought of the Open Air Campaigners, the Salvation Army, and the countless dedicated individuals who share Christ on their own. Our entire ministry, outside of my preaching, was on the street. It was what God had called us to in Chicago.

My heart broke as I thought of the hassles which lay ahead. We could not be denied this right to share Christ, especially since we never force anything upon anyone. Our ministry had to be preserved. We poured out our hearts to God, begging for an answer. "What do You want us to do? What *can* we do?"

God began to impress upon my heart that I should build a big wooden cross and take it to the civic center where I would pray and fast until our trial. I told M.

"Praise God," he said.

"Let's pray some more, M," I said. "I have to be sure God is leading in this." As I continued in prayer, I felt more strongly than ever that God was directing this vigil. I began to argue.

"Lord," I prayed, "You've promised me a boy, and he's due this month. I have to be with Tex during this last crucial month of her pregnancy. I can't leave her now. I can't."

I felt God telling me, "Sammy, you must. Sammy, you must." I knew deep within my heart that I had to do it. How I longed for my son to grow up in a country where he had the freedom to share Christ anywhere. I promised God my obedience.

In the wee hours of the morning, M and I found some lumber in the garage and built a crude, eight-foot cross. We brought it into my makeshift office and then went to bed.

In the morning M and I found the rest of the staff in the office, wondering what the cross was all about. Dwight, Lloyd and his wife, Gail, Tex, and Gordy Harbeck were there.

"I have to tell you what God has laid on my heart," I began.

Tex was with me all the way. She knelt next to me by the cross. The staff gathered around and put their hands on our shoulders and prayed for us. The burden welled up anew inside me. I thought of the countless ministries which would depend on the outcome of our trial. Tears fell from my eyes onto the cross, and I thought of the tears and blood Jesus had shed for a world which hated Him. I thought of Him dying there for my sin. A long month lay ahead.

I called the newspapers who had done stories on us in the past, and the word spread quickly throughout the news media. Surrounded by members of the print and broadcast media at the civic center, I explained our purpose in the vigil and fast. Lloyd and I were invited to several talk shows and were able to share Christ with a potential television audience of millions. We never let the current crisis overshadow our top priority: sharing the love of Christ.

After a couple of busy days, I sent out a newsletter to bring friends and supporters all over the country up to date. I asked them to send petitions to the mayor and the police department in Chicago, insisting that Christians be allowed to witness freely on the street.

We received tremendous support from all over. In the western suburbs, the Wheaton Bible Church held a twenty-four-hour prayer vigil for us, characteristic of many reports we received.

The First Baptist Church of Del City, Oklahoma, one of the largest churches in the Southern Baptist Convention, sent an official statement to Mayor Daley's office, protesting our arrest. They sent several prayer-grams to our headquarters, assuring us of their support.

The Illinois Baptist Association also adopted a resolution protesting our arrest and delivered it to the office of the mayor.

The office of United States Congressman John R. Rarick called from Baton Rouge to inform me that the congressman personally had contacted the state's attorney's office in Chicago to keep up to date on the case.

Petitions flooded the mayor's office. One day I tried to get in to see him but was, of course, denied. I introduced myself to one of his aides who said: "We know who you are. You're responsible for all these petitions."

We received calls from dozens of lawyers who figured our case would be a bandwagon to notoriety. The more I prayed about it, the more convinced I became that God wanted us to have a Christian lawyer. We waited for the right man. Meanwhile, our civic center ministry was in full swing.

The first person who came to Jesus as a result of our vigil was a man who talked with Lloyd. He prayed to receive Christ, then pulled a metal Playboy Club card from his pocket. He tore it apart with his hands, saying, "Man, I don't need this anymore."

As I sat on a bench by the cross one day, a girl sat down a few feet away. I looked up from reading my Bible. "Hey, do you know Jesus?" I asked.

"No," she said. "And I don't want to talk about it."

I never press the subject. I figure if a person doesn't want to talk or listen after I've opened the conversation, I have no right to continue it. I went back to reading my Bible.

After a few minutes, the girl turned to me with tears in her eyes. "I need help," she whimpered. She told me that she had run away from home and that the police were looking for her right at that moment. She said she had messed up her life.

"Jesus promised to give you abundant life," I said. She listened. I shared with her the testimonies of other runaways I had known and how God had saved them. "They still have the problems they had before they came to

Christ," I explained, "but Jesus has given them the strength to face their problems. Would you like to know Jesus?" Right there she prayed to receive Christ.

I told the staff members and the winos in the area what had happened and asked them if they could give a little money. Several of the drunks, who themselves had been begging, gave a few cents each and we raised enough to send the girl back home to the suburbs. It was the only offering I collected at the civic center. A few weeks later, the girl's mother came to tell me that her daughter truly had been changed. She thanked me for sharing the claims of Christ with her daughter.

A combination drug addict-pusher named Mike saw the cross one day while he was tripping. He thought he really was strung out and came over to find out if I was for real. He argued with me when I tried to tell him about Jesus, but he kept coming back, almost every day. I prayed that God would show Himself to Mike through me.

Mike was hanging around arguing the day an old man shuffled up. He was really ancient, hunched over, and limping.

"Are you a Christian?" the old man asked me.

"Yes, sir, I am," I said. He was hacking and coughing so violently that I wasn't sure he heard me. "Yes, I am," I repeated.

"Would you pray for me?" he asked. "I'm on my way to the Greyhound station to go home, and I'm not sure I'll make it." I knelt and prayed that God would heal the old man. Mike watched. When we stood, the old man straightened up, took a deep breath, smiled, thanked me, and walked off sprightly. Mike was floored.

"Wow!" he said. "I've never seen anything like that in my life. I want to know what you've got." We talked for

a while, and he prayed to receive Jesus Christ as the Lord
of his life. Praise God! Mike's life was radically changed.
He gave up drugs and went back home to the suburbs. He
joined us at several Bible studies.

The vigil fast was becoming one of the most beautiful
physical and spiritual experiences I'd ever had. I lost twenty-five pounds, but I felt in the presence of Jesus most of
the time. But I blew up once.

We had several well-meaning local Christians who often
joined us to help witness. One such man from a large
church in Indiana came one day and stood around hassling
the Blacks who came by. I had enough trouble winning the
confidence of Blacks without this professing Christian
standing there cutting them down and arguing. Finally, I
blew my cool.

I jumped off the bench, grabbed him by the shoulders,
and stuck my face close to his. "Listen here!" I shouted.
"You need to get right with God! You need Jesus to take
that hate and prejudice out of your heart and fill you with
love!" I let go; and he hurried off, obviously shaken.

He came back a few minutes later. I had been convicted
by God. "I still think you need to get right with God," I
said, "but I shouldn't have reacted the way I did. I want
you to forgive me."

Murray Bradfield joined me at the cross one night when
the drunks and winos were out in full force. I'd had many
opportunities to witness to them and had sent several over
to the Pacific Garden Mission. But when there were several around, I usually encountered nothing but chaos. This
night was no exception.

A Black drunk staggered up, fighting mad. He broke a
wine bottle and stumbled around with the jagged neck in
his hand, looking to cut somebody's throat. Everyone, in-

cluding Murray and me, kept out of his range until he threw the bottle away. Then he came over, grabbed Murray's hair in one hand and mine in the other and smacked our heads together several times, screaming that he wanted to kill us. We just kept shouting, "Jesus loves you, brother!" until he let go. Then we dropped to our knees and prayed for peace in the midst of the confusion.

One night at about nine o'clock I heard cheering and shouting in the distance. Suddenly a group of sixty or seventy Christian students from Moody, Wheaton College, Judson Baptist College, and local churches came around the corner. They carried Jesus posters and shouted "What does Chicago need? Jesus! What does Mayor Daley need? Jesus!" We had a great time of fellowship and prayer that night.

The ironic thing about their march was that they had walked down the sidewalks on Rush Street without any problems. Whereas two of us at opposite ends of the sidewalk were arrested for blocking pedestrian traffic, more than sixty of them had walked, some spilling into the street.

Finally, I received word from Moody Bible Institute that my case had been discussed at a meeting of the Christian Legal Society. I was given the names of several Christian lawyers who were interested in helping us. This was a real answer to prayer, especially since we recently had been contacted by the American Civil Liberties Union. They are noted for the great things they have done in cases for radicals, but I didn't want the public to get the idea that we fit that category. I would have defended myself before using an ACLU lawyer. I called George Newitt, a lawyer with offices near the civic center.

I was impressed with him right off the bat. The other

lawyers who had approached me all had been slick talkers and pseudo big shots. But Newitt sounded sincerely interested in talking with Lloyd and me. I told him that we just were genuine Christians who wanted the freedom to share Christ on the streets. "We aren't out to cause any trouble," I said.

After Lloyd and I had met with Newitt, he really became excited about the case. We took him to the scene, and he was sure we could beat the charge. The formal charge said that we had blocked the sidewalk (which was about twenty feet wide) and that we were guilty of disorderly conduct. Technically, disorderly conduct consists of three or more people causing a disturbance which results in a potentially riotous situation. Since there were only two of us, that charge was ridiculous as well.

Newitt really did his homework and kept us informed regularly on the latest developments. He took the case at no charge. That was the only way we could have employed a lawyer. Not only were we working on a tight budget, but God sent us four more staff members from Georgia during the vigil. It was during this time that I really marveled at how God had taken care of us materially.

A lot of food was donated to us. Once, God laid it upon the hearts of people at a church to give us 700 cans of various foods. We really lived on a tight budget. Our expenses ran close to $4,000 each month, and the Lord always laid it on the hearts of His people to provide for us. We have never violated our policy of not asking for funds. Another rule is that we give 10 percent to missions.

We finally got to the point where we salaried everyone according to his needs, but for a long time we paid salaries out of what was left after the mailing, literature, and other ministry expenses had been paid. Later, the total salary cost for eleven people was less than $600 a month. Our staffers really gave of themselves.

Murray and his wife joined us on a full-time basis during the vigil, as did two young men, Greg Stevens and Charlton White. By now the trial was just a week off, set for Wednesday, September 29, 1971. We planned a rally for Saturday, the 25th, at the civic center, but we didn't want to tell the news media until that day. We just spread the news by word of mouth.

Saturday morning it rained for hours, without a break in sight. But when the noon chimes rang in the United Methodist Church's Chapel in the Sky on the corner across from the center, the rain stopped. I praised God. About a thousand showed up for the rally.

Tex was past due about a week; and, as I continued to pray for her, it entered my mind that our son might be born on the day I went to trial. I churned inside, worrying about Tex and not knowing what might happen in court. I awoke Wednesday morning with a tremendous feeling of anticipation. For sure, this would be the heaviest day of my life.

Tex was in labor when I got to the house. By the time I left for court, Gail Cole was taking her to the hospital. I worried most about being out of court in time to be with Tex in the hospital.

My first stop was at Moody Bible Institute where Lloyd and I were interviewed on a morning radio show on WMBI. The host made a big deal of the fact that we wore ties and coats. This was the first time either of us had worn a tie in Chicago. But we weren't just a couple of radical kids, and the host assured his audience that our purpose was to serve Christ and to make Him the Lord of our lives.

After the show we went down the block to the studio of professional artist Joe DiValasco. Joe had offered us the place for a pretrial prayer meeting, since it was just a few doors from the police station. The *Daily News* quoted us as praying that the mayor, the judge, the state's attorney, and everyone involved would get saved. I requested prayer for Tex. About 150 friends joined us in prayer and then accompanied us to court, where a hundred others jammed the corridors. It was wall-to-wall people, many of whom I'd never met. My lawyer, George Newitt, already was there. The courtroom was packed.

Mr. Newitt had advised me to wear a coat and a tie, because the last thing he wanted was for the judge to be prejudiced against us. He wanted to get the case dismissed without a trial.

We waited while the judge ran through the cases of several drunks and vagrants. What was so sad was that these drunks were arrested every night, tried the next morning, and released. They would drop the charges, and the drunks would go back to the same old thing. Jail was just a place to sleep; they weren't being helped at all.

As I waited for our case, I suddenly heard the kids in the hall. "Give me a J! Give me an E!"

Oh, no! I thought. *Not a Jesus cheer now!* I was afraid to look at Mr. Newitt. I just hung my head and prayed. From the hall I heard, "What does the district attorney need? Jesus!"

"O Lord, no," I prayed. The news media was out there recording everything, and the police hustled out to quiet the kids down. I heard later that a secretary of one of the officers handed a staff member a check for $35, telling him that she knew we were being set up and that she was a Christian who was behind us. It really touched my heart.

City of Chicago vs. Tippit and Cole! A million things

seemed to race through my mind as I followed Mr. Newitt to the front. I clutched my Bible tightly.

Lawyer Newitt started boldly: "Judge, these boys were ticketed for passing out tracts. I think the case should be dismissed."

"No," the judge answered. "The officer claims that these boys have violated the law, and he intends to prove it."

"Then I want a jury trial," Newitt responded.

"Counsel, you are not entitled to a jury trial."

"Why not, Your Honor? These boys' constitutional rights have been violated."

"The law in this state says that, if the penalty does not require sentencing to a penitentiary, it is a misdemeanor and not qualified for a jury trial."

Mr. Newitt was shocked: "Your Honor, this is very fundamental. Do you mean to tell me that I can't have a jury trial on a question as vital as this? The Constitution sets forth certain rights as inalienable. If the Illinois law takes away this man's right to free speech and to exercise his religious prerogatives, then that law cannot stand."

The crowd was about to cheer, and the judge was scared by Newitt's statement. "I think I ought to have the city attorney here," he said. "I'm going to reserve judgment until he comes."

We left immediately, and our lawyer called his office to reaffirm his position on the law. Then he was surrounded by news microphones. "I felt like the President," he said.

When the city attorney arrived, he readily agreed that we had the right to a jury trial. The judge concurred, and it was set for October 13 in another courtroom. Then everything went up for grabs. Mr. Newitt, Lloyd, and I were surrounded by the press.

One of the reporters asked me if I had heard anything about my wife. Suddenly all the emotion which had welled up inside me for a month emerged, and I broke down. "No," I said, crying. "I haven't heard anything yet. I'm going to the hospital now."

"Sammy!" a voice yelled from the crowd. "You're a father! You've got an eight-pound baby boy!" Then the questions really started flying. I was drained.

"How does it feel to be a father?"

"I just hope my son is able to grow up in a country where he has the freedom to worship Jesus and to share Him with anybody he wants."

Greg Stevens had a car waiting, so I begged off, and we hurried over to the hospital. I was so excited I could hardly wait. I jumped from the car and ran into the hospital. "Which room are my wife and baby in?" I asked the nurse.

"What's the name, sir?"

"Tippit, Reverend Sammy Tippit. My wife just had a baby here."

"Mr. Tippit, there have been no babies delivered here. Debra Tippit is still in labor."

"What?"

The first thing Tex asked was how the trial came out. I spent the next several hours with her. It was a real lesson for me. I had no idea how much pain a woman could go through.

When she began to have terrific pains, I put my hands on her and prayed. She says that every time I prayed for her, the pain let up. Each time I said the name of Jesus, she felt that she went through less pain than she would have otherwise. Seeing her in labor drew me closer to her. I appreciated her more than ever.

At about five o'clock I took a break to get some chicken.

On my way back across the street to the hospital I picked up the *Chicago Tribune*. There, on the bottom of the front page, was the story of my going to trial and becoming a father on the same day. The story even carried my son's name, Paul David. For the first time in months, I thought about the possibility, after all of this, that Tex might have a girl. "Lord," I prayed, "what if I'm wrong?"

Then I felt ashamed. "Lord, I'm sorry. You've promised me a son, and I'm going to claim it." Tex's labor was prolonged. Nine and ten o'clock passed. I was scheduled for a television show at eleven. Gail was there, but still I didn't want to leave. Tex talked me into it. "You can tell a lot of people about Jesus tonight," she said.

When I left, she was in deep labor. I knew it wouldn't be long now. It was hard for me to concentrate while I was being interviewed, but I had a tremendous opportunity to share Christ. During a break at 11:30, a phone call came for me. It was the doctor.

"Sammy, I wanted you to be the first to know. You have a fine baby boy. A little over eight pounds." I really began to praise God. I went back on the show and told all about how God had promised us this son more than nine months before.

When I got back to the hospital, Tex was praising God. I finally got to see the son God had promised us. A fantastic day of emotional strain had ended for Tex and me. We just held each other and loved each other and cried. We had worried so much about each other. It was a sweet, unforgettable day.

The days between September 29 and October 13 were long and busy. Mr. Newitt had us draw a scaled chart of the nightclub area, and we really prepared for the jury trial.

George Newitt prepared the pretrial brief as if it were a

big deal, like a case he would try in the federal court. His young associate handled the case of Danny and Paul. He won an easy dismissal, but the boys were minors. Ours was a different case altogether. Newitt called the lawyer on the other side and told him that he should give up.

"If you go to trial," our lawyer warned, "you are going to lose. The city of Chicago and the police department are going to have a black eye. People are going to get the impression that all your policemen do is go around knocking citizens off the street when they are trying to pass out Gospel tracts.

"There has been a lot of publicity in this case. The best thing that could possibly happen to the city would be for the prosecution to let this case be dismissed and slink off into the background."

Newitt also told him that he contemplated filing a federal suit against Mayor Daley, the police chief, and the city for violating my and Cole's civil rights.

The lawyers representing the city never had run into a lawyer who prepared briefs, documented his case, and threatened to file counter suits. Our case had become a personal thing with our lawyer.

When the case was called and the judge asked if the prosecution was ready, the city attorney requested a continuance of an hour. Newitt knew then they were ready to quit. When you're going to fight, you answer, "Ready, Your Honor," our lawyer explained. But instead, the prosecution asked to meet with the defense.

We went to the office of the chief enforcement attorney for the city of Chicago. He was a tough, cocky guy. He conducted a mini-trial all of his own and then lectured all who were involved. Mr. Newitt knew all he was doing was trying to save a little face, but he got to me.

"Would you stake your life on the fact that LeRoy had a switchblade?" he asked.

"Well, I'm almost positive because I saw him flip it, and it had a long blade."

"Long? How long? You're not sure? LeRoy, what did you have in your hand?"

"Fingernail clippers," LeRoy said.

"No," I said. "I know the difference between a knife and fingernail clippers." He was trying to make me look ridiculous.

"Let's say he did come after you with a knife. You didn't have a right to tell the police, did you? Why did you want to cause trouble?"

"Don't I have the right to report it to the police when I'm threatened with a knife?"

"Did he touch you?"

"No, but he came at me—"

"See? You had no right. You don't know how we live around here. What you should have done was sock him in the nose."

"I don't believe in that." He was trying to make me look like a dumb hillbilly who'd found himself in the big city. "Sir," I said, almost in tears, "if you think I'm lying, then I'm willing to go to court. Let's just go ahead." I didn't just want the charges dropped; I wanted the freedom to witness on the street. This guy was just playing mind trips, hassling with little words. It broke my heart that in America, government is run this way.

Newitt whispered to me, "Now knock it off. We're going to get out of this all right. We've got them over a barrel and they're giving up."

"Well, I'd rather have the trial," I said. "I want to go to trial and prove that I'm innocent."

Newitt insisted there was no need to go to trial. We agreed not to file a federal suit against the officer, and the city agreed to drop their charges.

I didn't know if we really had gained our freedom or if we had just played a little game with them. I didn't realize how big a victory we actually had won until we were threatened again a couple of weeks later. I went to the district commander. "We've been threatened by a nightclub owner again," I said. "We don't want to hassle you people, and we don't want to go through a big deal again."

"Don't worry, Tippit," he said. "I'm issuing an order that none of my men are ever to arrest you boys when you're out there telling people about Christ. If more young people were doing that, I wouldn't have half the problems I have today."

Lawyer George Newitt felt good about the outcome. He said to us: "We gave the city a whipping. The personal satisfaction I received from defending the rights of Christians to share their faith without intimidation will last much longer than any payment I could have received."

7 / Dope, Demons, and Confusion

It was good to get back to the Uptown streets and reestablish friendships with kids who had come to Jesus through our ministry. Our Bible studies were booming, and I had several more opportunities to share Christ on such local television shows as "Of Cabbages and Kings" and "Kennedy and Co."

In a three-day period we received over a hundred letters from kids who'd messed up their lives in drugs or the occult. I believe that the drug revolution of the late 1960s paved the way for satanic influence such as the occult. I received several letters from a fifteen-year-old guy from Rockford, Illinois, named Allen, who had been having what he described as terrifying, ugly visions. When I went to Rockford for a week of meetings, I got a chance to talk to Allen in person.

Allen had been doing hallucinogenic drugs while listening to hard rock music. In an attempt to lessen the horrifying effects of the visions, Allen switched to tripping with softer music in the background. Sure enough, his visions changed. One night while freaking out, he saw the face of a man on his pillow. It made him think of Adam.

Next he saw the face of a woman, and he thought of Eve. The next image was a combination of the first two, and he thought of love.

"Allen, do you love me?" To Allen, it was unmistakably the voice of God.

"Yes, Lord," he said, "I love You."

"Would you do anything for me?"

"Yes, Lord, anything."

"Allen, will you give yourself to me?"

Allen was excited, certain that God was talking to him. "Yes, I'll give myself, Lord. How can I do that? I want to give myself to You."

"If you love me, Allen, you'll kill yourself."

Allen found a razor blade and slashed his wrists several times. The blood gushed and splattered up into his face. He collapsed. He came to for a split second and saw a vague image of a cross. Then he was out again.

Allen's father found him just in time to rush him to the hospital and save his physical life. For a year psychiatrists worked with Allen to no avail. They tried to convince him that he was deluded, that he had not heard a voice. When Allen came to me, he was desperate.

"No matter what anyone says," he said, "I know I heard the voice of God. People tell me I'm crazy, but I know what I heard."

"I don't doubt your experience," I told him. "And I don't doubt that you heard the voice of a god. But I know without a doubt that it was not the voice of the true and living God, Jehovah, Jesus Christ. My Bible tells me that Jesus came to give life, not to give death. The Bible says that Satan is the god of this world, and I believe it was he who talked to you.

"Through drugs you have opened your mind to demonic influence and satanic powers. You can be set free right now by the power of the blood of Jesus Christ if you will repent of your sins and trust Him."

"Sammy," he said, "if this was of Satan, I want to be delivered from it. And I want to be delivered from dope."

I laid my hands on Allen; and, while he prayed to receive Christ, I prayed that God would perform a miracle in his life and change him. I rebuked the power of Satan in his life in the name of Jesus. Nothing emotional happened, but since that day Allen has lived for God.

Kids are finding that they can experience highs and hallucinations without drugs. They're beginning to freak out on the occult. I was shocked when I first began to encounter Satan in physical ways. Every Christian needs to know that Satan is a very real person and force today. We can only minister to messed-up lives if we realize that Satan is the one who traps minds. Many of the kids who are into the occult openly worship Satan. They aren't being subtly tricked; they're being lied to. A girl came to the house one night and told me that she loved Satan. "If my lord knew that I was here in a Christian house, he would be very angry," she said. "I don't know why I disobeyed him and came here."

I doubted whether or not she was for real. So I started reading from the New Testament about the cleansing blood of Jesus. As I read about His blood being shed on the cross, the girl shrieked. She drew herself up and curled into a human ball. "Don't read that," she hissed. "Don't read any more!"

"What's wrong with this?" I asked. "This is the Word of God." I reached out and touched her with my Bible. She cut loose with a bloodcurdling scream and backed into the corner as if she were trying to climb the wall.

"Please don't touch me with that," she begged. "Oh, please don't!"

"In the name of Jesus I have the power to denounce

Satan in your life," I said. She cringed and whimpered.
"But you have to be willing to denounce him." She clawed
at her face, crawled on the floor, and quivered. The more I
talked about the blood of Jesus, the more agony she went
through. When I stopped and talked about something else,
she snapped out of it and became very intelligent and ar-
ticulate. She never did denounce Satan or let me rebuke
his power in her life.

A few weeks later I ran into an even more bizarre situation. A girl who had witnessed with us two years before
in New Orleans came to see me in Chicago. She had been
a professing Christian. But since I had seen her last, she
had gotten into a freaky religion in Chicago which claimed
to worship a four-person godhead consisting of Jehovah,
Lucifer, Satan, and Christ. She claimed to love them all.

"Donna," I said, "don't you see that Satan has lied to
you? He has deceived you into thinking that you have found
truth. God can deliver you." Then I prayed, "God, give me
wisdom and show me how to pray."

The next thing I knew, I prayed that God would force
the demons in her body to identify themselves. I had no
idea that she was possessed, but God laid it on my heart
to pray this way. I didn't know of any particular sin she
was into besides this Satan worship.

"No, no, no, no, no," she said. She shook her head violently.

"In the name of Jesus! Demon, you have no authority!"
I shouted. "I command you to identify yourself!" She sat
shaking her head. "I'm not playing games," I said. "I come
on the authority of Jesus of Nazareth who died, was buried,
and who rose again and is coming again!"

"Sex!" she screeched, and everyone in the house fell si-
lent. Staff members dropped to their knees. I commanded

the demon of sex to leave her body. She pulled her hair
and clawed her face and then fell limp. The demon had
been cast out. But I didn't have a peace about it. I felt
that there might be more.

"If there are any other demons in Donna's body, I command you in the name of Jesus Christ to identify yourselves." The demons of false theology and deception were
cast out, as were several others. At one point she shouted,
"I hate Jesus." I repeated the procedure five times, and
each time demons were cast out.

As I continued to pray, Donna became maniacal. She
wiggled on the floor like a snake and finally began to
screech at the top of her lungs, *"Lust, lust, lust!"*

"I command you in the name of Jesus to come out!" I
shouted; and again she fell limp. While she lay on the floor,
I commanded three more demons to identify themselves
and to leave her. Finally, ten demons had been cast out.
"If there are any more demons, I command you in the
name of Jesus Christ to identify yourselves," I said. When
she lay still and didn't respond, I said, "All right. In the
name of Jesus, you have been set free."

"No, no," she said.

"I said in the name of Jesus! Didn't you hear me? In
the name of Jesus, what is holding you back now?"

She went into a worse fit than when the demon of lust
had been revealed. She jumped up, screaming and shouting
and pushing things over. She grabbed at anything near her
and flung it, whirling around and crashing into the furni-
ture. It took four of us to hold her down.

"Whatever demon is holding this girl, I command you
in the name of Jesus Christ and in the power of His shed
blood to identify yourself!"

She almost broke loose from our grasp. She kicked and

scratched and screamed: "Satan! Satan! Satan himself! I love Satan! He is my lover, and I will not let go of him!" She had been willing to get rid of the demons because they were tearing her mind and body apart, but when it came down to ridding herself of Satan, she wouldn't do it. We started singing "Victory in Jesus," and she joined in with a squealy, mocking voice.

"Donna, in the name of Jesus, I command that you denounce Satan," I said. I repeated the command several times, but she refused. "Then, because in the past you have claimed the name of Jesus, you are hurting the testimony of the name of Christ. I have no other choice. I now turn you over to Satan for the destruction of your body in due time in the name of Jesus." I acted upon the authority of 1 Corinthians 5:5, "To deliver such an one unto Satan for the destruction of the flesh, that the spirit may be saved in the day of the Lord Jesus."

Donna came to on the floor. She was in one messy room. "What in the world happened?" she asked.

"Don't you know?"

"No."

I told her, and she continued to insist that she could love Jesus and Satan at the same time. "I don't give you long to live," I warned. "If you ever had a true experience with Jesus, He cannot tolerate this."

When my son was as young as six months, he didn't sleep well after the staff had engaged in discussion about demonology. Once I tried to read about Satan to the staff, and Davey started crying. When I stopped, he stopped. When I began again, he cried again. It was weird. Several times I tried to begin, hoping it was just coincidence. But it wasn't. We often pray over him and claim the blood of Jesus to keep Satan from hassling him.

It surprises me how many churches have problems with satanism. Of course, most church people really don't want to encounter Satan; but, when they mess around with Ouija boards and seances, they're asking for trouble. I know people who have lifted tables without touching them, and who have seen little horns fly around the room. No, it's not their imagination. It's the very real power of Satan.

Demons often come in the name of Christ, though their power comes from the devil. The Bible says that Satan comes as an angel of light, but Jesus is the only true light. If you don't know whether or not a "fun" evening is right or wrong, try a simple test. Is anyone coming to Christ? That's what the whole Bible is about, but it never happens at a seance or a Ouija board party.

I believe Satan is trying every trick in the book because we're in the last days. Christ is coming soon, and Satan doesn't have much time. I'm shocked at the number of church young people who are "innocently" messing around in fortune-telling, astrology, and witchcraft. Satan will give them power, but they will pay the price (see Luke 10:18-20).

On the other end of the spectrum, some people are hung up on demons. They'll cast a demon out of every tree. When there is a demon, God will give us the power to cast it out; but just because sin is evident doesn't mean a demon is present.

Many do not believe that Satan can produce imitations of the gifts of the Spirit. I know he can. Every good, holy, divine gift can be reproduced by Satan in fleshly form. One day a young man came into our Chicago ministry and said that he wanted to know Christ. I told him that he needed to repent of his sin and turn in faith to Jesus Christ. I asked him to pray and receive Christ into his life.

"Dear J——" was all he got out. He fell on the floor in a fit, similar to an epileptic seizure. I had the eerie feeling that he was filled with the power of Satan. I called the staff in to pray for him. Connie McCartney, who had been delivered from speed and Satan worship, gasped when this guy started ranting in an unknown tongue. It was unknown to all of us but her. He used the same words she had used years before in worship of Satan.

In the name of Jesus, I commanded the demons to leave his body. He fell limp. God showed me that certain tongues certainly can come from Satan.

Not once have I sought the gifts. Not once. I believe that this is a vital point. To seek a gift is an abomination unto God. Seeking the gifts is not a New Testament concept. We are to seek Jesus, Jesus alone. When we make Him the Lord of our lives and let Him deal with sin and self, then He will pour out His Spirit.

Don't seek experiences. Seek Christ. There are enough people hawking experiences, happenings, and zaps from heaven. Jesus will distribute the gifts the way He wants to. We can't go around telling everyone which experience they should have or which they are entitled to.

Something frightens me about the Jesus Movement. Many Jesus People say, "Let's get high on the Spirit. Let's get high on Jesus. Let's have an infilling, a baptism of the Holy Spirit. Jesus is groovy." But while they are pushing the highs, they are not dealing with sin and self. I repeat: there cannot be a genuine infilling of the Holy Spirit if sin and self are not done away with.

I was asked to speak at a Jesus festival once, and I got turned off. While the band blasted away at a song with unintelligible lyrics, kids lifted their hands, gazed into heaven, and praised God. It was blasphemous. The kids didn't even know it, but the band was playing a secular song. The kids had been physically turned on by the big beat, and they figured the band was praising God.

Girls in mini-skirts stood and raised their arms toward heaven, causing the guys to lust. Some young girls come to our meetings in short skirts or hot pants, and I have to pray to stay in the Spirit. It breaks my heart to see so little conviction of sin in the Jesus Movement. I believe in taking the love approach, but there has got to be conviction of sin. People have to get right with God and get their hearts cleaned out.

The Bible says that a person must confess his sin and turn from it. Confessing is agreeing with God about sin. It's saying, "God, I've been wrong." Sin can be broken into two major areas: sin against God and sin against your fellowman. God will not pour His Spirit into an unclean vessel. In our ministry, we have noted that a real outpouring of the Spirit always follows great conviction of sin. I've seen kids throw away dope, adults throw away booze and tobacco, and all ages burn dirty books and witchcraft paraphernalia. When the conviction, confession, and repentance take place, God pours out His Spirit in a mighty way and not in some weird, sensual experience. This was borne out one Sunday at the Maplewood Baptist Church in Cahokia, Illinois. I had prayed all morning that God would burn a message on my heart for that evening, but nothing came. Finally, during the song service just before my sermon, God impressed it upon me just to ask for testimonies.

Hands went up all over the auditorium, so I said, "Let's pray and ask God to choose who He feels should come and give a testimony." A half-dozen people came to the pulpit publicly to confess sin and get things right with God and their neighbors. The Spirit had moved upon that congregation. They had received a baptism of love. But it couldn't happen until the people had dealt with the sin problem. Dozens came when the invitation to receive Christ was given.

I've seen people who preach in the name of the Holy Spirit but who are on nothing but an ego trip. I've asked countless evangelists to counsel me, to tell me the secret of their ministries. The first thing they talk about is finances. "Don't be afraid to hit people for money. Make sure your expenses will be taken care of." I don't buy it. The secret to our ministry is "broke-ness." Oh, we need "broke-ness."

God will not despise a broken heart and a contrite spirit, says the psalmist. A lot of people cry out for the Spirit but aren't willing to come broken before God. Often in my ministry, people say, "Sammy, you're doing such a great job. You're winning people to Jesus and helping young people." The minute I start to agree with those who pat me on the back, God withdraws the power of His Holy Spirit from my life. The Bible commands me to be filled with the Spirit. I can't be filled unless first I'm empty. Empty of pride and empty of self.

Being filled with the Spirit is not some spooky experience. It happens when the Christian gets sick of himself and sick of his sin. The Holy Spirit comes to glorify God the Father through Jesus the Son. So when we're Spirit-filled, we should praise and glorify God. I want to be a man totally possessed by the Holy Spirit. I will always seek the Giver and never the gifts.

8 / *With God in Germany*

The idea that God wanted me someday to preach behind the iron curtain had led me to sign up for Russian language courses in college. Each time, however, the course had been full, and I was bumped into a German class. I never could figure that out. I didn't want to take German, so I dropped each course, wondering why God wasn't opening the door for me to learn Russian. I found out in the fall of 1971, after the excitement of the vigil and trial had mellowed.

When Arthur Blessitt visited Chicago that summer, I again felt the spark of interest and divine leading to a ministry behind the iron curtain. In fact, I began to see Chicago as a microcosm of the world in its sin and degradation, an example of how Satan unleashes his power on every continent. That summer I went to Trinity College in Deerfield, Illinois, to train counselors for the Blessitt rally in Chicago. No one showed up for the training; but as I waited, I noticed that the only thing in the room was a map of the world.

I fell to my knees, and God began to lay deep impressions on my heart for some type of a world ministry for Jesus Christ. "God," I prayed, "I'll do anything to further Your Kingdom." I felt I needed to talk to Arthur, but I was afraid that his advice would be to stay in Chicago. I hopped in the car and headed for Homewood, Illinois, where he was supposed to be staying at the Holiday Inn.

I got off the interstate at the wrong place and just drove around, hoping to find the way back on. I saw a Holiday Inn, so I decided to stop and get directions to their place in Homewood. As they checked a map for me, I mentioned that I was going to see Arthur Blessitt. "Blessitt?" they said. "He's not in Homewood. He is staying here." God had led me right to him.

"Lord," I prayed, "speak to me through Arthur."

Arthur was excited. "Man, if that's what God is telling you to do," he said, "you'd better do it." As we knelt to pray, I knew God was fixing to open a worldwide ministry for Jesus through "God's Love in Action." I wasn't sure exactly what it would be, but there was no doubt that God planned a heavy thing for our lives.

We had had little time to plan an overseas trek while the trial and vigil were on. But when everything had blown over, I came back to the streets of Uptown and my world burden began anew. Murray Bradfield and I often stayed up until the wee hours of the morning, praying that God would show us distinctly what He wanted us to do world-wide.

One morning at three o'clock, we were on our knees alone in my little office. We felt impressed that God wanted us to walk across Germany for Jesus. In college, God had tried to prepare me by having me take German; but I was so ding-a-lingy, I wasn't listening to Him.

As we got down to the nitty-gritty preparations, we saw that God would have to deal with three major obstacles. The first was that we didn't have the money—no bread to go. We felt that to be effective, we should take our singing group, "The Living Water." For transportation alone, we would need twenty-five hundred dollars.

Second, we had no contacts in Germany. We knew of no one who could set up speaking engagements and accommodations for us.

Third, we couldn't speak German. Murray had a year of German in college, and I should have had several. It was a lesson to me that when God tells you to do something, you'd better do it.

We felt led to go in December of 1971. That didn't give us much time. As December approached, we sought the face of God. "Lord," we prayed, "we have to know. If You want us to stay in Chicago, we'll stay; but if You want us to go, we should be getting our visas and reserving flights. Lord, we need twenty-five hundred dollars."

That very day, a man came to the house. He was a schoolteacher. He had saved money for years; but that morning as he prayed, God had touched his heart, and he felt led to come and give us a check. He had no idea what our financial need was, but God did. The man handed us a check for twenty-five hundred dollars. We really rejoiced. We had a blessed time, sharing with the man how we had prayed for that amount.

I received a list of English-speaking churches in the European Baptist Convention. On it was the address and phone number of each pastor. At random, I called a pastor in Germany. I told him that we felt led to carry a cross across Germany to symbolize Christ as the answer to that nation's crises. He discouraged me; I guess he thought the idea sounded far out. He offered no help.

Two weeks later, he called me. He had seen news releases and magazine articles about our ministry. Now he was excited about the possibility of our coming there. He asked if I first would speak at a retreat in Austria for pastors from all over Germany. That would take care of the contacts. God blessed, and the doors were swinging open. From there I hoped that we would be able to set up a schedule of meetings and stopping places along the way.

Murray and I got to work, studying German as quickly as we could. By the time he and I and Charlton White were ready to go to Austria, we were fluent enough to try out our German on the stewardess. We had a blast, finding out how close or how far we were from the actual pronunciations. We prayed and witnessed and sang all the way, but God had even more in mind to help us communicate.

In Mittersill, Austria, the pastors had a real love and real burden for revival. They opened up to us, and we had a wonderful time of prayer and inspiration together.

Murray and Charlton stayed in Germany after the Mittersill retreat to set up meetings and plan the walk while I returned to the United States for last-minute preparations. We planned to walk from Munich to Kassel, and Murray and Charlton had no trouble lining up meetings for us between those cities. But we did face two more hassles.

The first was that we still had no contacts in Berlin. I wanted to hold a prayer-and-fast vigil and rallies there and call all of Europe back to God. Without a contact, things looked dim.

The second hassle was that we needed another two thousand dollars. We found that Germany's electricity is not the same as in the United States, so our group's sound equipment was no good over there. We needed all new equipment and a van to carry it in. As soon as we realized how great that need was, money began to pour in from all over. We simply trusted God to provide if this trip was in His will. It was and He did. We sent two thousand dol-

lars to Germany; and when we arrived, a van and sound
equipment would be waiting for us.

The group was anxious to go, and I was happy to be able
to take Tex and Davey with me. I dug out the $72 my
friends had raised for me several years before, and we
looked forward to fueling the spark God had instilled in me
during my college days. We left for Germany on November 28, 1971.

"Sammy Tippit? Sammy Tippit?" The accent was that
of a German. I knew no one in Frankfort! "Sammy Tippit?" For sure, that's what he was saying. I turned around.
A sharply dressed man in his late twenties smiled at me.
"Are you Sammy Tippit?" he asked.

"Well, yes, I am," I said, a bit rattled.

"My name is Volkhardt Spitzer," the German said.

"Well, great," I said. "That's nice."

"I've heard of you," Spitzer said. "Our church in Berlin has been praying for you since your arrest in Chicago."

"How did you know me?" I asked. We were stopped
over in Frankfort, waiting for a flight to Munich. The last
thing in the world I expected was to be known in Frankfort.

"You looked American," he said, "and when the girl
[Tex] said 'Sammy' in an American accent, I wondered if
you could be Sammy Tippit." I told him that we had been
praying for a contact in Berlin. "Don't worry about that,"
he said. "I'll arrange a rally for you with the German people. We'll have several thousand there."

God had miraculously directed Volkhardt and me together. He had been on a nonstop flight from Berlin to
Munich, but was rerouted and his plane stopped in Frankfort. We were scheduled for the same flight to Munich. We
spent the entire time planning for a Berlin rally. Volkhardt's

church was large and well known; in fact, it was nationally publicized for its extensive youth outreach.

Murray and Debbie Bradfield were supposed to meet us at the airport in Munich, but they weren't there. We were welcomed, however. The German press was waiting for us. Volkhardt interpreted for us, and we were able to share our burden and faith with the news media that first day. Murray and Debbie finally showed up. It had taken them two hours to drive less than thirty miles because they hadn't yet learned to read the road signs.

We had planned a rally for December 1 in a huge theater auditorium on a United States base in Munich. We started early, setting up our new sound equipment and planning for the big crowd. An hour later, after "The Living Water" sang, I preached to a crowd of three adults and five teens. The devil really hassled us. I got a few minutes into my message, and three of the teens walked out. I was shaken. "Lord," I prayed silently, "have we blown it somehow?"

What I didn't know was that the kids who left had gone to all the bars and halls on the base and rounded up a bunch of GI's for the meeting. By the time I finished I had an audience of about twenty young people. Four or five got right with God that night, and we praised Him. The next two nights the crowds were much larger and we started really to see results. One of the chaplain's daughters came to Christ, and several Bible studies were begun at the base.

Our first personal contact with the Germans came at the University of Munich when Murray and I went there to witness. I was scared to death, praying that God would give me the words to say and help me to understand what the Germans were saying.

The Marxist party was in control of the student government and the communist leaders of the country were pictured all over the walls in the student union. It was an eye-opener for me. Communism dominates the whole way of life over there. Communistic pictures, posters, and literature abounded.

Two guys of several I witnessed to prayed to receive Christ. They understood only a little English, so it was my quoting of Scripture in German which made the difference. They got involved in a Bible study group on the campus and began to grow in the Lord.

As we were leaving the university, I stopped to talk to a girl. I handed her a sticker which read "Real Peace Is Jesus."

"Nicht Jesus," she said. *"Zondern Marx."*

I knew only a little German, but God gave me the words to say. *"Marx ist tot,"* I said. *"Jesus lebt noch."* (Marx is dead, Jesus still lives.) The Word of God pierced her heart, and her face fell. Later I thought about the importance of what I had said.

After our last rally at the American military base, we left the city limits of Munich at midnight for our walk. Ahead lay our main destinations of Augsburg, Stuttgart, Frankfurt, Giessen, and Kassel. Our wives would wait in Munich until we were close to Frankfort. Then they would go to Frankfort in time to meet us. From there they would go to Kassel where we would meet them after the walk.

Murray and I walked the first six kilometers (about three miles). The rest of the guys drove ahead and waited for us. Then we alternated and rested in the van while two others walked their six kilometers. It snowed as we walked, and it was beautiful. Again we were interviewed by the press as we entered the city.

That night we were to speak for the first time to Germans in a meeting. I had never used an interpreter while

preaching, and I was nervous. The meeting was to be held
at the Augsburg Evangelich Frei Kirche (the Evangelical
Free Church). We hadn't slept, but we were excited about
this first German meeting.

We were warned not to be too loud or get too excited or
give an invitation. We were told that the typical German
is very sophisticated, intellectual, and formal. We prayed
for strength and wisdom.

An hour before the meeting, the place was packed and
people were still coming. When all the seats were taken,
lines still formed outside. People stood in the aisles, by the
walls, filled the vestibule, and spilled into the hallways.
People, people, people on top of people.

Murray had set up all the German rallies, and it became
obvious that God had given him wisdom in the planning.
The Jesus Movement had received wide coverage in Germany, so many people were curious to see what we were
all about. But mostly, we attributed the large crowd, here
and all along the way, to the work of the Holy Spirit. God
was moving upon the Continent.

As I preached that night, I had little idea how I was
being received. It seemed that some of the people were
intensely interested, and our music or jumpy style hadn't
caused anyone to walk out. Then I got to a sentence which
stumped the interpreter. He paused, trying to think of a
German word. Before he could get it out, several men,
sitting on the edges of their seats, blurted it out for him so
I could continue.

That night about thirty young people responded to the
claims of Jesus Christ. In the prayer room, those kids
prayed with real earnestness. They weren't emotional or
psyched up. They talked to God as a friend. They con-

fessed sin and really repented. It was refreshing to see such honesty.

The next morning I spoke to the entire student body of the local *hochschule* (high school). I was allowed to say anything I wanted. I preached extensively on the claims of Christ and what He could do for a young person. I concluded, "If any of you would like to turn from your sin and give your heart to Jesus, I'd like to meet with you right now in this corner."

To my utter amazement, more than half of the student body rose and started moving toward the corner. "Wait," I said. "Just a minute. Let me explain this more fully." I went through all that it means to be a follower of Jesus. I didn't want it to sound "in" or cool. I explained that it meant sacrifice and discipline and dedication. Again I asked those interested to come to the corner. Again more than half started to move. "OK," I said, "I'll have to talk with you all at once, right where you are."

Up to this time we had noticed little conviction of sin in Germany. Promiscuous sex was widespread among young people, and they seemed to have no second thoughts. But now, as I explained the forgiving power of Jesus, kids started to ask, "Is this wrong? Is that wrong?" It was hard for us to leave as kids swarmed around us asking question after question about the Christian life. These kids were starving for the Word of God.

We had a long walk ahead to Stuttgart. We stopped to eat at a little meat market just outside Augsburg. I bought a loaf of bread and chose a couple of packages of wurst. It really was good.

There were a few things we grew tired of. One was wurst. Another was two sleeping bags in the van that really got raunchy. It was terrible. We'd climb into those things with our muddy feet after miles of walking, and they got to reeking something awful. It got to the point where I'd sleep in the cold before I'd even touch them.

We called our van "Aby Baby," after Abraham's stepping out on faith. Riding in Aby Baby was really stepping out on faith.

God had provided that rickety old van, and we thanked Him daily for it. But sometimes it really was frustrating. The only way we could start it would be to push it and pop the clutch. We had some hilarious times when it would stall in the middle of a downtown street. We'd all jump out and off we'd go, running and pushing with Aby Baby spitting and popping and rattling and shaking. It was better than having nothing to ride in, and the wurst was certainly better than going hungry. God met our needs.

The trip continued through one outpouring of God's power after another: through Fellbach, where, before we ate, we stood and each turned to the one next to him and said, "I love you in Jesus Christ, and may God's blessings be upon you"; through Mannheim, where, with little publicity, almost fifty kids expressed a desire to make a commitment of their lives to Christ; through Frankfort, where we experienced a tremendous time of revival in an English-speaking church; through Neuisenburg, where a plot by the Communists to take over the service was turned into a great outpouring of the Holy Spirit; through Giessen, where God shamed us into realizing one conversion could result in a Bible study which now averages sixty kids each morning; and through Kassel, where we had great Christian fellowship with some Lutheran and Evangelich deaconesses.

The time drew near for a prayer-fast vigil at the Berlin wall.

The train had trouble with its heating system, so we had

to wrap Davey in everything we could find. As the train moved from West Germany to East Germany, border guards came and checked our passports and luggage. We made it through with no problem. We were just praying that the rest of the staff, in Aby Baby, would make it.

Oh, Aby Baby must have looked a sight! On top of that old rattletrap was an eight-foot cross, a lantern, and an old spare tire, probably worse than any of the four on which Aby Baby bounced along. We prayed that the German guards wouldn't find the suitcase full of Bibles and tracts. Some vehicles were searched for hours at the border, but not Aby Baby.

Murray told us later that everyone was ordered out of the van and the guards began their search. The guards could hardly stand the stench from those rank sleeping bags, so they hurried. The first suitcase they popped open was Murray's. A whiff of one of his stinky undershirts sent them scrambling out of the van with an "OK, go on."

We contacted Volkhardt Spitzer who took us out for breakfast and found us a place to stay. He put us up in a beautiful three-bedroom cabin on a lake. It really was peaceful and scenic.

We set up our prayer-and-fast vigil in downtown Berlin at the Wilhelm War Memorial Church. We prayed and witnessed beneath our cross, and many German Christians came to join us. We had many opportunities to share Christ there and at our rallies each evening. Our second evening rally was broadcast on nationwide television, and the Lord really used the opportunity we had to glorify Him before the entire country.

On December 24 I prayed with a German girl who wanted to know Jesus. It was very difficult because I had to pray in German. I didn't know whether or not she got saved because she prayed too fast for me to understand. She was from a family of believers named Schoch, and they invited us over that evening, Christmas Eve.

In Germany, Christmas Eve is a very important family night, so it really was a miracle that they invited outsiders. When we arrived, the daughter was bubbling over. She had gone home and sewn on her sweater, *"Jesus liebt dich"* (Jesus Loves You).

Finally, God opened the door for Murray and Debbie and Tex and Davey and me to go behind the iron curtain. A young American Christian who was studying in West Berlin was going to visit some of the underground Christians I'd read so much about. A law says that no home can entertain more than three people in one evening unless it is an announced birthday party. With our guide, there were six of us. So, we went two by two.

We went to the home of an old gentleman. When our guide introduced us as Christians from America, the old man greeted us with a big bear hug, tears in his eyes. He had studied English for just six months, but he put us to shame. He spoke English more fluently than we spoke German.

He had been the pastor of a Lutheran church, but had refused to sign a document penned by the communist government. The document stated that Jesus Christ was the Son of God and was a savior, but not *the* Saviour of the world. By signing the document, the man would have agreed that Communism was the savior of the world. The Communists had removed him from his church. He was a heartbroken old man. He put his life on the line to stay there and send letters to all of the Lutheran clergy, urging them not to sign the document. None of them complied with his request. He was the only one who had stood up for his belief.

His children had turned on him as well. They were going to communistic schools where atheism was taught. Our hearts broke with his as he shared the difficult conditions under which he lived. The Lord showed us a real need behind the iron curtain, and we assured him that we would share this need with praying Christians in America. God really is moving, and at least some Christians are taking a stand there.

On Christmas Day Tex and I went back to Berlin and prayed at the wall. The wall took on a real spiritual significance as we stood there. I saw it not only as a barrier lined with machine gunners and mines which separated a city, a race, a people, a nation. I saw it as a wall which separated people all around the world—the wall of sin, the wall which separates people from God. My heart tore within me; and I prayed, "O God, we must be closing in on the last days."

The next day, as we stood out of the rain at the War Memorial Church, the cross was stolen, almost right before our eyes. It was out of our view for only a few moments; but the next time we looked, it was gone. We couldn't imagine anyone walking off with an eight-foot cross in downtown Berlin. It was as if God said, "I've given you a cross to bear, and now I'm taking it."

After visiting with Volkhardt that day at his church, I walked back to the War Memorial Church. It was chilly and damp, and I was thirsty. I stopped on the way to get some hot chocolate. As I sat there, I looked out through the windows of this totally glassed-in restaurant. People all around me spoke in German. Then it all came back to me. The glassed-in restaurant, the people speaking a for-

eign language! I looked at their faces. They were the faces
I had seen in my vision three years before. The Spirit of
God came upon me and thrilled me. The Lord had given
me one more sign to assure me that the walk and the worldwide ministry were just a part of His plan for "God's Love
in Action."

As we boarded the plane for Chicago the next day, I
thought of the old man in East Germany, the communist
students, the loving brothers and sisters in Christ, and how
the Holy Spirit had blessed our walk and our meetings. I
knew that one day we would return as God worked through
us in a worldwide outreach. We left Murray and Debbie
there to carry on the ministry and planned to return in less
than a year.

We were greeted in Chicago by many friends who were
anxious to hear about our trip. It was good to be back, but
I began to realize that God was directing us away from
Chicago. He had led us to discontinue our Bible studies
and to let them be handled by the new converts we had
made disciples. God had multiplied our ministry, and ten
Bible studies had grown out of ours. The streets were being taken care of with Christians witnessing regularly.

During a week of meetings in Miami, Florida, I learned
of the demonstrations planned by the radicals for the Democratic National Convention. God impressed upon me that
the convention would be an ideal place to witness and demonstrate for Jesus.

While speaking in May at a church in East Gary, Indiana, God laid it on my heart to make a walk from Orlando
to Miami, beginning a week before the convention. As I
fulfilled final obligations in the Chicago area, Tex and several of the staff went to Miami to set up our office and
apartments. We were excited about the future.

The morning that I felt led to plan the march I received a call from a pastor in Orlando who said he would help set up rallies along our walk route through southern Florida. God had given us a tremendous burden and now an opportunity to call America and its leaders back to God.

9 / Crossed-up Convention '72

We were in the midst of a four-day crusade, and I was at the home of the pastor of the First Baptist Church of Fairfield, Illinois, when Greg Stevens came to the house. "I've got some news, Sam," he said. "George Wallace has been shot, and he may not live."

I could hardly believe it. I was stunned. Greg repeated the news and we switched on the television. I'll never forget the feeling I had as I watched and rewatched Wallace being shot and falling to the ground. Mike Sutton, our pianist, joined Greg and me, and we fell to our knees in prayer for America. We begged God to pour out His Spirit on the country and to bring America to its knees.

We thought of the irony of all the politicians assuring via television that their prayers were with the governor and his family. Arthur Blessitt had challenged all the presidential hopefuls in the first primary in New Hampshire to make a definite public statement about their personal faith in Christ. None did so. But now they prayed.

That night in the service the Lord led me just to share the burden I had for the country. We prayed for Governor Wallace and his family and others close to him. God broke me in public as He never had before. As I prayed, I fell to the floor, weeping and crying out to God to move upon America and restore its sanity.

I preached on the need for a real spiritual awakening on a personal as well as a national level. God called sixty Christians to a more definite commitment that night, and twenty sinners came to Jesus.

Later I shared with Greg about the time I had spoken to Governor Wallace about Jesus being the answer to the crises in America. We prayed that if he lived, he would remember that and turn everything over to God. If he died, we prayed that God would bring that witness to mind in time for him to make sure of his standing with Christ.

I had said nothing to the press about our plans for Miami; but, when we left the Fairfield crusade, I saw a St. Louis newspaper which had quoted me. Someone had sent out some news releases quoting me as saying that I was going to bring between 700 and 2,000 Christians to Miami to blitz the radicals and to put them in their place. It said further that I planned to split the radical camp and get them saved.

It was true that we were concerned about confronting the radicals with the claims of Christ, but we were just as concerned with witnessing to the straights, the politicians, the right-wingers. A couple of religious periodicals implied that physical force might be used by Christians against the radicals. We were not associated with any such plans, and I was afraid that these charges, along with the Wallace shooting, would just add to the tension between the conservative and radical groups in Miami.

I worried about Tex and Davey, who already were in Miami. Radicals already had been arrested and hauled off the beach and into jail. I called Tex from Chicago following the Fairfield meetings. I told her not to let anyone know, except local Christians, that she and Davey were even in town. We prayed together over the phone, and I also instructed her to make no statements should the press contact her.

Having witnessed on the street and having enjoyed rapport with young people, I knew the general attitude of the radical group. Being from the Deep South and having shared Christ with the conservative and even so-called redneck adults, I was aware of their general attitude as well. Both sides are vocal, prone to physical violence, and very passionate in their beliefs. In my mind, the possible confrontation was as potentially dangerous as it could be.

I felt that "God's Love in Action" would be right in the middle of any confrontations at the convention, since we would be trying to work in and among both groups. The conservatives wouldn't like our looks, and the radicals wouldn't like our associating with the red-necks. We just wanted both groups to know what Jesus had to offer. The only way the radicals and the red-necks ever will get together is if both turn their lives over to Jesus Christ.

We weren't going to Miami to side with any group politically. We had put our political feelings aside and would ask people to seek Jesus first.

I've wept at night as I've prayed for this country I love so much. I felt it was time for something drastic to take place. The passages of 2 Chronicles 7:14 and Joel 2:15, 21 came to my mind again: "If my people, which are called by my name, shall humble themselves, and pray, and seek my face, and turn from their wicked ways; then will I hear from heaven, and will forgive their sin, and will heal their land," and "Blow the trumpet in Zion, sanctify a fast, call a solemn assembly. Fear not, O land; be glad and rejoice: for the LORD will do great things."

I still had some meetings scheduled in Vandalia, Illinois, before the march to the convention, but I felt it necessary to go to Miami first to be sure our strategy was set. We planned to have a staff man with a cross at the headquarters of each major candidate. I hoped to be stationed inside the convention center with a cross.

We talked with a Major Schuller in Miami who was in charge of demonstration permits. He OK'd the crosses in front of the campaign headquarters of McGovern, Humphrey, Wallace, and Muskie, but he referred us to the Democratic National Committee on the request to have a cross inside the convention center itself.

We explained to the Democratic leaders that we planned simply to tell people about Jesus and pray with them if they wished. We would pass out tracts and hold a vigil at each cross to demonstrate for Jesus. A young official with the national committee sympathized with our position. "I respect you," he said, "and I believe that you have the answer to the problems of our nation. You've really got something going, and I'll do everything I can for you."

We got a promise from the police that they would arrest no Christians during the convention, but the security heads were forced to deny my request to have a cross inside the center. I heard from Leo Humphrey in New Orleans, and he agreed to join me on the walk when I reached West Palm Beach in July. Bill Hartseil of The Barn coffeehouse ministry in Peoria, Illinois, also would join us, as would several other key leaders from street ministries. Many kids planned to come as a result of publicity at Explo '72 in Dallas. We really started to get excited about the possibilities.

On Saturday night, June 25, Satan began his thrust in Miami. One of the major hotels hosted a rock opera about Satan worship. I felt led that we should carry one of our crosses around outside the hotel and witness to people as they went into and came out of the place. While the performance was in progress, we prayed that God would make people physically sick of Satan. He did.

Several of those coming out of the hotel made statements such as "Wow, that made me sick. I don't want to have any more to do with that!" People were very open to our witness.

Each night we went to the convention center to pray. One night the police removed us from inside the fence, explaining that someone had cut the fence away from twenty-six poles. It appeared to be an attempt by radicals to gain free access to the convention center. Thousands could have scooted under the fence in its sabotaged condition. The snipped wires were hard to detect, but from that day, every inch of the four and a half miles of fence was under constant police surveillance.

Tension began to snowball. Ten different groups of protesters announced their involvement, including the Gay Liberation Front, the Southern Christian Leadership Conference, Vietnam Veterans Against the War, Yippies, and their offshoots, the Zippies.

In Dade County, the Ku Klux Klan had burned seventeen crosses. Another right-wing group claimed that if Miami opened up to the radicals, they would bring thousands of KKKers, hard hats, and red-necks into the city to break up their campsites. The city council worked furiously, passing tougher laws against obscenity, vulgarity, and inciting violence.

I didn't know yet if it was from God or not, but I began to have a feeling, a premonition of personal disaster. I couldn't shake the idea that something might happen to me during the convention. I didn't want to have fear in my heart, and certainly I didn't want to have a martyr complex. But the feeling made me stop and think, *What am I doing for Jesus every second? Every moment, every breath must be Christ living through me.*

Tex and I discussed what would happen to her and Davey if they were left alone. I wrote a list of things which would need to be taken care of, should I be killed. I didn't enjoy thinking this way, but it was something which constantly plagued my mind. I couldn't turn tail and run from the convention or any potential danger now. I knew God wanted me there and that it would be the greatest opportunity our ministry had ever had. My burden for our work grew, despite the premonition. It lay deep and heavy on my heart.

After a meeting in Vandalia, Illinois, I flew back to Miami. Lloyd picked me up at the airport, filled my tired body with coffee, and hustled me to a press conference at the General Development Corporation. Fred Roach, the president of the company, hosted the media for us.

Some members of the press had tried to make us look like just another bunch of freaks into some kind of a weird trip. So we prayed that if there were any press people who wouldn't glorify Jesus, that God would not let them come to this press conference. We would rather have no coverage than bad coverage.

The three top media showed up. The *Miami Herald* and two television stations quizzed us. Everything was so Christ-centered and God-glorifying that we were able to share the claims of Christ with the entire city in the paper and on TV. One TV newsman was so excited about what we were doing that he gave more air time to us than he did to Jerry Rubin.

Rubin was leading the first Yippie demonstration the next day, so we prayed to see what God would have us do.

As it turned out, there were more secret servicemen and newsmen than demonstrators. We infiltrated the march and witnessed and passed out tracts. The demonstrators figured we were passing out antiwar literature; but, even when they found out that it was Gospel tracts, we had some good discussions.

I confronted Jerry Rubin with the claims of Christ. He said nothing. I got the impression that he was afraid to face himself or God. I think he also was scared that we were going to turn his people to Jesus and blow his whole impact apart.

The next day I was scheduled to speak at the Kiwanis Club. It was an opportunity that only God could have given. But I had just twenty minutes to speak and then rush to the airport. I had an engagement to speak in Orlando before the eight-day walk to the convention. God gave me the strength to come on strong with the Kiwanis, and I was encouraged by their standing ovation as I hurried to the car in which Lloyd rushed me to the airport.

We were greeted by the local press when we landed in Orlando at three o'clock that afternoon. The first guy who interviewed us was a new Christian. He asked all the right questions, and we were able to share how to be saved.

Over 700 people showed up for our 7:00 P.M. rally at the Orlando band shell. A Black girl sang a cappella, just like Ethel Waters. It was beautiful. Greg sang and led some singing, and I preached. Several kids came forward and prayed at the foot of the cross. We shared the details of the walk which would begin near midnight. Several joined hands in a circle and prayed for us. We surrendered our lives anew for the glory of God. Before we left, we witnessed to a lot of bad dudes, including a car thief who got saved and even was directed to a church to attend.

Greg, M, and Bob West, a new Christian from Sparta, Illinois, would join me on the walk, perhaps the most important in our ministry.

July 1, 1972

The first leg of the walk, starting near midnight, took us through the Black section of Orlando. Greg and I walked first, and Bob and M drove ahead in the van. The recent cross burnings by the KKK made things rather tense, but we had so many opportunities to share Christ that this wound up as one of the longest parts of the trip.

A number of people had heard about us in the news, and some even came to walk with us for awhile. We walked until 10:30 in the morning and covered just thirty-two miles. And we got eaten up by mosquitoes.

We walked almost due east through Melbourne, Florida, where we would turn south and head straight for Miami. I had a lot of time to pray as we walked during the wee hours, and we felt the very presence of God on our beings.

We could hear snakes and came across several snake carcasses in the road. We were pretty wiped out when we finally stopped to rest for awhile, but we had to make it to Haynes City by evening for a rally sponsored by area churches.

There was tension between the longhairs and the straights at the meeting, but God blessed. Greg led the singing and I preached. Several came to Christ. One of the pastors came to me later and asked my forgiveness. "I judged you because of the length of your hair," he said.

July 2, 1972

At about 4:00 A.M. Greg and I took our break and drove a couple of miles ahead of M and Bob. We were sleeping soundly when a knock came on the door. M stood there with a real sharp-dressed guy. I was groggy and confused. "Where's Bob?" I asked.

"He's still back there walking," M explained. "This guy drove me up here on his cycle. I've been witnessing to him. He needs Jesus. Sam, can you talk to him?" After I stepped out to talk to the well-dressed cyclist, Greg got up and drove M back to where Bob was walking.

"Would you like to know Jesus?" I began. I quickly realized that the guy was totally drunk. He didn't say much, and I figured something was wrong. I suddenly felt very alone with this guy. We went over to his 600 cc cycle, and he bent over the saddlebags. I kept talking.

Suddenly he turned and pointed a long-barreled gun at me. I ignored it at first. "Will you pray with me?" I asked. He cocked the gun.

"I don't want to pray," he slurred. I knew he meant business, and I thought my premonition was coming to pass. I thought of Tex and Davey and of all the things which would have to be done if this guy blew me away. But I still couldn't figure out why he wanted to kill me. I wasn't scared of dying, but the situation frightened me. My knees shook, and I prayed as I continued to talk about Jesus.

"Put on this holster," he ordered. I figured he'd want it to look like I was the one who had the gun. "If anyone drives up," he said, "you just tell 'em we're havin' a friendly talk."

Greg pulled up and the guy hid his gun. "It's OK," I said, "it's just my friend, Greg." As Greg walked up, the drunk pulled the gun out and fired it. Greg and I jumped. Each thought the other had been shot. Neither had. Down the road, M and Bob heard the shot and didn't know what was going on. They stepped up their pace.

"That's the wrath of God upon you," the cyclist said. "That's power, power!" He put the long-barreled gun in the holster which I'd strapped on. He pulled out a hand gun and challenged me.

"I don't like guns," I said, unbuckling the holster. "Let's put it up." He took the holster and the long gun and put them away but kept the hand gun. I finally talked him into putting it away and praying with me. He was totally irrational, but he knelt with me.

When Bob and M reached us, we were still on our knees. I motioned for them and Greg to get in the van. I kept talking to the guy. He stood up and went to his bike and started it up. I sprinted for the van and sped off. He was reaching in his saddlebag again as we drove off.

We drove twenty miles before we saw any sign of life. Finally, at the intersection of Interstate 95 and route 192, we stopped at a Holiday Inn and called the county sheriff. He sent out some officers to take a report, and we stayed there until daybreak. At about 6:30, we drove back to where we had stopped walking and began again. It was hard to forget that night and the husky gunman.

After a few more hours of walking, we drove to Winter Park, a suburb of Orlando where Tex had given her testimony in the morning service at the First Baptist Church. We slept at the home of the director of evangelism, Miles Riley, until 4:30 in the afternoon.

We awoke to find that Bob and Greg had blisters so bad they couldn't continue. Luckily, Bill Hartseil showed up from Peoria with two members of his staff, Lewis Riggenbach and Steve Thorson, who filled in on the walk. Bill drove Greg and Bob on to Miami to help set up the convention ministry.

At the service that night the pastor called the deacons together to pray for me. I felt the power of the resurrected Saviour, and God anointed me anew for the walk. It really blessed my heart. I had to leave during the invitation to get to a radio station in time to be on a show. I was curious to know if anyone had come forward to receive Christ or to get right with God, and I found out soon enough. The radio show continued for two hours, and many people called in who had been at the service. We were thrilled to hear how many had been blessed.

July 3, 1972

We walked all night and saw the sun come up. It was beautiful to hear the sounds of the ocean on our left. As the sun rose in the sky, the heat was almost unbearable and took its toll on our bodies. All I could think about was getting some rest. I was really wiped out. At about 11 o'clock in the morning some guys stopped to give us a cola. Many people along the way had heard about us on the news, and we had several opportunities to share Jesus.

We figured the wire services had picked up the story because we were seventy miles out of Orlando and still people knew who we were. Finally we stopped at a state park and tumbled to the grass under a tree to sleep in the shade. It felt so good to stretch out.

As the hours passed, the sun moved. So did the shade. I woke up at about 7:00 P.M. with a terrible sunburn, another move of Satan. People warned us about the rattlers, so we changed routes a bit to get out of the snake area. We praised God for giving us clear nights with no rain when we could walk. The days were just too hot for much walking in the afternoons.

July 4, 1972

I looked through the newspaper to see what was the latest in Miami with the radicals and their camping. I found nothing about it, but I noticed a headline which read, "Spiritual Change Nation's Only Hope." "Praise God," I said and started to read it. I was shocked to find that it was my own testimony, in the first person, telling explicitly why we were walking and what we were all about. It even quoted 2 Chronicles 7:14. The publicity had been super.

We walked twenty-six miles, and I had two things on my mind. First, Greg and Bob were going to witness to the radicals at the golf course in Miami, and I was anxious to hear how it went. Second, I missed Tex. My heart ached to be with her and Davey. I thought about them constantly and prayed for them often, conscious of the fact that I might not see them again. It seemed that this was the most dangerous walk I'd been on, not just because of the political tensions but because every time we turned around, something popped up.

We stopped at another state park in the afternoon, and I called Lloyd to see how things were going. He said that twenty-five radicals had been housed in a synagogue and only fifteen camped out at the golf course. "God's Love in Action" had almost as many people witnessing at the golf course as the radicals had camping out!

July 5, 1972

Just after midnight we passed by a place called the Royal Castle. The place was jammed with longhairs who came running out to see what we were all about. It wasn't every day that a van and two guys carrying a cross went by. They couldn't understand what we were doing, and they asked a million questions. So, right there in the parking lot, we held a service. It was really fantastic.

At about 3 o'clock in the morning, the sheriff advised us not to continue our walk until daytime. There had been a prison break and several convicts were loose. By stopping in the van every so many miles, we were sitting ducks for guys who would need hostages and wheels. So we stayed in a hotel until the next afternoon.

We contacted the local news media in West Palm Beach to tell them that we would arrive the next day for a rally. I really got excited because this was where Leo would join us.

We left, walking again, at about 4:30 P.M. The first thing that happened was that a reporter and a photographer from the *West Palm Beach Post* came out to do a story and pictures. We really gave them a story, including the story of Jesus.

That night as I walked, I felt the power of the Holy Spirit in my life. Oh, He was ready to do something. I didn't know what, but I was filled with expectancy. I looked at the skies, and I knew that the One who created the stars and the lakes and the whole beautiful universe lived in me and desired that I glorify and praise His name among all nations. I thought of the blessed promise in the Bible that He will give us the nations for our inheritance.

July 6, 1972

As day broke, we again were visited by the news media. This time, three television stations, two newspapers, and a radio station interviewed us. The coverage had grown, and God protected that mode of witness, making sure that all the reports were accurate and contained a solid word for Jesus.

In West Palm Beach we contacted Fenton Moorehead, director of Love One Another ministries. He is the former youth director at the First Baptist Church of West Palm Beach and was able to find us a place to rest before the night's big rally.

I had gone hours without sleep, but for some reason I was too psyched up to rest. Tex came at around 3 o'clock, and it was great to see her.

Earlier we had prayed with the Reverend Charles McKinney, a turned-on pastor from Oxnard, California. During prayer, God impressed me that if, besides myself, we could get just ten real men of God to work together in Miami, we could really shake the convention for Jesus Christ. We still had a long walk ahead, but we trusted God to send us four more godly men.

Already I would work with Leo, Lloyd, Greg, Bill Hartseil, Bob MacDonald, and Fred Bishop, a pastor from southern Illinois. So many times Christians get hung up on numbers, but Jesus used just twelve disciples, and just a few men at Jericho, and relatively few with Gideon. Every time God worked, He worked through the faithful few.

During the rally we let a representative of the Christian World Liberation Front share his testimony. As he shared, he happened to mention that the CWFL would have its four top men in Miami to work with us if they were needed. We praised God for rounding out our ten!

The spirit was fantastic in the service. The kids were all over the place, and many came to know Jesus. Christians got right with God. Several news reporters were there, and again we were able to glorify Jesus in the press. Things were building for the convention, but Satan hadn't given up yet either.

We got word from Miami that Lloyd and Fred Bishop

had an opportunity to witness to and to pray with Ralph Abernathy, head of the Southern Christian Leadership Conference. Lloyd had prayed aloud in front of him, "Lord, don't let Abernathy do anything in the convention that You don't want him to." We knew the Lord was working. The staff had already had many chances to share Christ with radical and political leaders. Praise His name!

July 7, 1972

We made it to Fort Lauderdale by 10 A.M. and made last-minute plans to arrive in Miami in twenty-four hours. It was good to hear that the park was proclaimed, by the radicals, as the people's park where anyone could come and do anything or say anything he wanted. That meant that we could take our cross and our tracts and our preaching in there. We looked forward to it.

I shared a little at the Fort Lauderdale rally, and then Leo preached. Again, several were saved. We felt that, if nothing happened at the convention, the walk and the revival blessings of God would have made it worth the effort. We couldn't wait to get back on the road that night, because our next stop was Miami.

We had only twenty miles to walk, but it was obvious from the start that we would walk all night. Many people stopped us and talked with us; we had heavy raps all along the way. The closer we got to Miami, the more often we were stopped by the police. Every so many miles we were stopped and questioned. It was good to know that security was so tight.

July 8, 1972

At about 3:30 A.M. we moved inside the Dade County limits near the town of Bal Harbour. FBI agents stopped and questioned us. They had nothing against what we were doing, but they feared for our safety. So, until we arrived at the convention center at 10:00 A.M., we had an FBI escort. On the way the agents had Leo come into the car for about a half hour, then they asked me to join them. We had wonderful opportunities to witness, and the agents were excited about what we were doing.

As we neared the convention center late in the morning, we stopped to pray in front of Hubert Humphrey's headquarters. The secret servicemen out front were a bit freaked out. They didn't know what to make of an eight-foot wooden cross and demonstrators who didn't cause any trouble. McGovern's headquarters were also on the way, so we stopped there too.

By 10:00 A.M., when we slowly moved into the convention center, about twenty-five Christians, including Tex and the staff and many other brothers and sisters in Christ, met us for a prayer meeting. We prayed that God would cleanse us and use us for His glory. I felt led that we should walk around the entire center with the cross, praying and praising God. Symbolic of when the walls of Jericho fell, we decided to walk around the center once each day and one extra time to make seven, calling on God to smash the walls of sin.

With that first trip around the center with our cross and our Lord, we officially began our ministry in Miami and the Democratic National Convention.

In the afternoon, Ralph Abernathy called a press conference at Flamingo Park, so I thought it would be a good chance to see the people's park. We didn't see much of Abernathy or the SCLC, but the "people's park" sure was an eye-opener. It was like a big rock festival. There were tents, and every group had its own little place. Everyone did his own thing. Some just ran around like maniacs. A girl lay naked on the ground. Another group had a marijauna smoke-in. "Let's go get the cross," I said.

Fred Bishop and I brought the cross back from the convention center, but we didn't get fifteen yards inside the people's park before we were mobbed. Freaks, newsmen, everybody flocked around, and the questions really started to fly. Network TV men and both wire services were there, and we gave a solid statement on our purpose of calling the country back to God through Jesus.

The cross quickly became a controversial item. Some people were drawn to it while others were turned off totally. Some said, "Wow, this is beautiful. What're you guys doing?" We had great chances to witness. The Yippies displayed their characteristic hypocrisy by trying to kick us out of the people's park.

We decided to walk through the park, approach no one, pass out no tracts, and do no preaching. We let interested people come to us. And scores did. A Yippie said, "You can't stay!"

"Why not?"

"You're contrary and controversial, and you're not preaching what everybody believes here!"

"Well," we said, "Jesus loves you, and this is the people's park." Leo looked the guy in the eye and told him he loved him, and the dude walked away.

After a few hours of sleep at home, we gathered to finalize our convention strategy. All the guys met with us who were to be stationed somewhere with a cross. We made the following assignments: Just outside the convention center would be Leo and myself. Greg Stevens and Bob Mac-Donald would be at Wallace's headquarters. At Humphrey's headquarters would be Bill Hartseil and Lewis Riggenbach. Lloyd and M would be at McGovern's headquarters. Jim Rich and Steve Russell, two old friends, would be at Muskie's. Fred Bishop and a number of staffers would be at Flamingo Park.

At 6:00 P.M. we had a prayer meeting with all the guys and prayed God would move powerfully and affect the convention by our presence. We figured that the crosses would blow everybody's minds, especially the news media. Every time they moved to a different candidate's headquarters, they'd see the cross. And when they got to the convention center, they'd see it again.

July 9, 1972

I went to church and had a blessed time in prayer for revival. The convention was to begin the next day, so the Miami Baptist Association sponsored a prayer rally at Lumnus Park. Jack Sparks of the Christian World Liberation Front and Jim Ponder, director of evangelism for the Florida Baptists, spoke. I shared our burden and asked everyone to join in a mass circle for prayer.

Then we marched to the convention center and made our second walk around the grounds. As we prepared to leave, we heard yelling from down the street. Thousands of freaks moved our way, shouting, "The pope smokes dope! Marijuana now! Marijuana now!"

As they got to the front of the convention center where we were, they stopped marching but continued to chant.

"Praise God," I said. "Jesus now. Jesus now. Jesus now." The Christians picked up on it. "Jesus now. Jesus now. Jesus now." TV cameras whirred and tape recorders spun. "Jesus is the answer! Jesus is the answer!"

Then we regrouped, and I said, "Let's form a circle around their demonstration and point your index finger to-

ward heaven (signifying one way). Don't say anything
unless someone says something to you, and then say only,
'Jesus loves you.' And pray." As we split up, we prayed
that the power of God would encircle the demonstrators.

One of the demonstrators shook his fist in my face.
"We'll get you Jesus Freaks!" he said. "If you Christians
break up our demonstration, we'll get you!"

"Jesus loves you," I said, smiling, finger pointed aloft.
We heard favorable comments from newsmen and spec-
tators, but not from the demonstrators, needless to say.
The Lord blessed in a fantastic way, and the demonstrators
finally left in disgust. We knelt to pray for their salvation.

I spent some time with Tex and Davey in the evening.
At midnight, Leo and I would begin a fast-and-prayer vigil
at the convention center which would last until the convention ended. We prayed that, outside the convention
hall at least, Jesus Christ would be the major issue.

With just snatches of sleep here and there during convention week, I still remember the entire time as one long
day. Things were pretty quiet at the convention center cross
that first morning, but at about 3 o'clock two homosexuals
stopped by to talk to Leo and me. They became our first
converts at the vigil. "Man," one said, "I want to be set
free from this homosexuality. It's eating me up." We
prayed, and God set them free. We got their names and
addresses so we could follow them up.

Each morning at 10 o'clock we made our daily walk with
the cross around the convention center. Often we were in
the right place at the right time and wound up in the middle
of tense situations. More than once we found ourselves
between two rival groups. We would walk back and forth
between them, praying and singing and witnessing. God
cooled down the demonstrators time and time again. We

feel that He had as much as anything to do with keeping the entire week peaceful.

When we'd kneel to pray in the middle of a potential riot, people from both sides would come, assuming that we were in some kind of a sit-in, and ask, "What's happening here?"

"Jesus is happening here," we'd answer. We got countless opportunities to witness, and several people came to Christ. There were many witnessing groups in Miami, and I don't suppose we'll ever know how many people were led to Christ. Through "God's Love in Action" alone, we had between fifteen and twenty each day who prayed to receive Christ and asked to be followed up by our staff.

Each night we held what we called a soul session where we sang, cheered, witnessed, and preached. One night we were interrupted by a demonstration by the Gay Liberation Front. They marched along, staging a kiss-in. It was really gross. What disgusted me most was their leader, a gay pastor who preached the blood of Jesus. That's a dangerous, blasphemous thing to do. I confronted him.

"The blood of Jesus has cleansed us," he claimed.

"What about repentance?" I asked.

"We have repentance."

"What about your homosexuality?"

"We need not repent of homosexuality," he said. "It's not a sin. Jesus and the disciples were gay." My stomach turned. To think that this guy was advocating homosexuality in the name of Jesus!

"I rebuke you in the name of Jesus Christ of Nazareth," I said. "Brother, you're going to burn."

That evening, Leo and Bob MacDonald and I went to a restaurant for some coffee, our main staple while fasting. We passed out tracts and, without knowing it, Bob gave a tract to Ralph Abernathy. Lloyd had mentioned my name to Abernathy the week before, so he recognized it on the tract. Tears filled his eyes and he asked if we would pray for him right there in the restaurant.

We laid hands on him, and Leo prayed aloud that he would get right with God, really let Jesus be the Lord of his life, and see that the only solution to the problems in this country is to win souls to Christ. I really believe that God is working on his heart, convicting him that he should preach the Gospel of repentance and faith in Jesus rather than a social, political gospel. The future of Christ's Kingdom in this world may depend in a large part on such Black people and whether or not they'll turn back to God.

The next day the Zippies held a mock convention rally. They had a wheelchair with a dummy of George Wallace in it. While they shouted peace slogans and insisted that the bombing and killing end in Vietnam, they fired a blank gun at the Wallace dummy and threw it and the wheelchair over the fence.

We carried our cross around them, and some of the radicals got up-tight. "Look!" they shouted. "We don't want you guys around here anymore! You're ruining everything!"

"We're here," I said, "because Jesus is the answer. Not violence and hate." We didn't back down one inch.

After a tense rally one night, in which we sang "We Are One in the Spirit," the SDS gathered about a thousand people to demonstrate what they called "true democracy."

"This is the people's mike," they shouted into their public address system. "Anyone who wants can come and say anything they wish about anything! We'll show the world what true democracy is!"

We prayed about it, and Leo stepped up to the mike. He began to preach Jesus. "No, no!" they screamed. "We don't want to hear you!" They tried to take the mike away from him, characteristic of the type of democracy they advocate. They want a democracy as long as you agree with them. Some of their rank and file realized that they were violating their own stand, so they said, "Let him speak!"

The other radicals shouted, "Get him off the mike!" Division had come to the radical camp. We were on our knees, begging God to let Leo speak.

"I challenge you!" Leo said. "You've tried everything else in the world to solve problems. I challenge you to pray with me right now!" It blew their minds. Then he gave the plan of salvation and handed the mike back to them.

Some said, "Man, that's heavy. He's really got something."

Others said, "We ought to kill those _____."

That night I preached with the power of the Holy Spirit at the soul session. Scores of people literally swarmed around us. I preached repentance; the death, burial, and resurrection of Jesus; spiritual revolution; and Jesus as the only hope. We had as big a crowd as any of the demonstrations. People responded to the invitation by the dozens.

I got reports daily on what happened at the other cross stations. On the day that Humphrey announced his withdrawal from contention, Bill Hartseil hit his knees and prayed for a chance to witness to the senator. Later, when Humphrey came out, surrounded by a human ring of secret servicemen, Bill prayed, "Lord, open the door for a witness."

For no apparent reason, the secret servicemen's chain broke momentarily and Bill stepped in next to Humphrey, seemingly unnoticed. "Sir," Bill said, "I just want you to know that we're praying for you, and that Jesus loves you. He's the only hope."

"I believe you, son," Humphrey said. "I believe you." Bill stepped away, and the secret servicemen locked arms again. As Humphrey's limousine drove off, the senator stared back at the cross until it was out of his view.

Lloyd Cole reported that he ran into David Brinkley of NBC television news and shared Christ with him and left a tract with him. That same night someone handed Lloyd two floor passes to the convention for "the guy who's carrying the cross." Praise God. We turned it over to Jesus and prayed that He'd direct us to whomever He wanted to witness to inside.

Leo and I got to witness to several national leaders on the convention floor by just approaching them, introducing ourselves, and telling them about Jesus. I heard that a certain governor was a Christian, so I approached him.

"Governor," I began.

"Yes?"

"My name is Sammy Tippit."

"Yes?"

"I understand that you're a born-again believer in Jesus Christ."

His mouth fell open. He said nothing.

"I've heard that you have Jesus in your heart and that you know Him as your personal Saviour."

Still a blank stare.

"Haven't you met Jesus?"

His mouth hung open and he tried to speak.

"Sir, are you a Christian?" I asked.

"Ah, uh, ah, yes, I guess so."

"Well, great," I said. "I represent the Christians outside

who are proclaiming that Jesus is the only hope. I'd like to challenge you, if you really know Jesus, to take a definite stand and publicly say so." I handed him a tract.

"Ah, well, thank you, son," he said and hurried off.

Come to find out, I had the wrong governor! But God knew what He was doing. I never would have had the nerve to even approach that governor if I'd known he wasn't a Christian. I'm sure I gave him a lot to think about!

The next morning, while the guys were marching around the convention center, I tried to see Wallace and McGovern. I met with Wallace's brother-in-law who relayed the message to the governor. The word was that the governor wanted to meet with me, but that security regulations and medical problems made it impossible.

At the McGovern headquarters, I wound up in the middle of another fracas. The state troopers came in after getting wind of a plot by radicals to take over the place. They shoved people in and out until the thing finally broke up. As I stood there, watching the radicals acting like babies, shouting obscenities, and carrying on, I almost wept. My heart ached for revival in personal lives. I walked around there for hours, praying that God would save these kids who cursed Jesus and the national leaders.

M, who had spent a lot of time at McGovern headquarters, witnessed to a girl who was starved for love. She had been shacking up with some of the Vietnam Veterans Against the War and did not lack for sex, but she was sick of being used. All the guys wanted her for was her body, but she wanted genuine love. M told her about the most perfect, ultimate love of God in Jesus Christ. M took her to Leo, and she prayed with him to receive Christ.

We figured all the action was at McGovern's headquarters; but meanwhile, at Flamingo Park, another confrontation was in progress. We had arranged for a North Carolina singing group, "The New Directions," to sing at the park. During their performance, the radicals stormed the stage, hit one guy in the stomach, grabbed the mikes, and took the drummer's sticks. But six big Black guys from the SCLC intervened.

They jumped to the platform and threw the radicals off. "If these dudes wanna sing about Jesus," they warned, "you let 'em sing!"

One of the Yippie leaders made a statement to the press that day. "Man, these Jesus People have got it all together. At first I wasn't afraid of them, but they've thrown this whole thing into chaos. Everywhere we go, there they are, at the campaign headquarters, at the park, at the convention, everywhere. We can't do anything. We've got division. I'm not blaming the Jesus People. It's our fault. We gotta sit down and talk with them and find out what they've got. They've got it more together than we have."

We had been praying that the main issue *inside* the convention would be Jesus. But it wasn't. *Outside* the convention, however, Jesus was the whole thing. The radicals didn't know how to handle us. Most of them were infuriated; but some, praise God, got saved.

On Thursday afternoon, I got a chance to preach in Australia and Russia. The bureau chief for a big paper in Sydney interviewed me for his syndicated column which was to appear in newspapers, magazines, and radio stations. I shared that we believe that Christ is the only hope of glory.

Another guy interviewed me and began to translate in a foreign language I didn't recognize. Then it came to me. He was from the Voice of America broadcast and was translating my witness for Jesus in Russian for listeners behind the iron curtain. Praise Jesus! God had opened the door for a worldwide outreach in just a few moments, all because we simply trusted Him with our lives.

That night I met one of the most unusual personalities I have ever run into. His name is Hubert Lindsay, but he is called Holy Hubert. Just five foot six and 135 pounds, Hubert is a ball of fire you either love or hate. There's no middle ground with Holy Hubert.

This fifty-seven-year-old street preacher has been hospitalized a dozen times after getting beat up, shot, and stabbed in demonstrations where he'd tried to preach. He's fearless. I was down on his methods at first, but God taught me a lesson through him. I have never seen anyone with such compassion, wisdom, and boldness from the Holy Spirit. He was something else. We were having a prayer meeting with him when he spotted a bunch of Vets Against the War sitting by a dike they'd built. "I'm gonna stir 'em up a bit," he said, with a twinkle in his eye.

He wasn't as crass as he appeared, but he knew what he was doing. Basically he was drawing a crowd. "You filthy, rotten sinners!" he started, shaking a finger at them. "You're headed for hell. Your souls are black—"

Boy, I want to tell you, a crowd started to gather and old Holy Hubert really began to preach. He changed his tone a little and really used his head. He preached Jesus and Him crucified and from a crowd of almost 300, someone tried to put him down. Holy Hubert got a special dose of wisdom from the Holy Spirit.

"Hey, man!" the heckler shouted. "Why don't you blow a little grass with us? God created marijuana, didn't He?"

Never missing a beat, Hubert shouted back, "Yeah, God created poison ivy, too. Why don't you chew a little of that?" The crowd cheered.

"Well, I'm gay!" another yelled out. "I believe God wants people to be gay!"

"You're not gay," Holy Hubert countered. "You're queer. Gay means to be happy; and no queer is happy, because only Jesus makes you happy."

Two other hecklers challenged Hubert with questions about Judaism and Buddhism. Hubert knew more about the history of their religions than they did. Just then the Zippies came through, about a thousand strong. Hubert just kept preaching to his crowd.

There was real confusion. The Zippies shouted into their microphone, and Hubert was just as loud without one. The Zippies tried to carry him off, but the crowd protested. About sixty of us Christians walked through the mass and sang, "Just as I Am."

We eased the attentive crowd off to one side, and Hubert and I alternately preached. The Holy Spirit fell on that place in a mighty way, and people got saved.

Some of the radicals really took to old Hubert. They said, "This guy's got more guts than any of our guys." It was true. God impressed me with Hubert's holy boldness. In Hubert's history was an incident with a Hell's Angel who had shot Hubert and was then sent to jail. After Hubert recuperated, he bailed the Hell's Angel out of jail and led him to Christ.

After our seventh walk around the convention center, we began to praise God for the revival He had sent, for the opportunities we'd had, and for the growth in each of our lives. We went home and immediately started a follow-up program, mailing encouragement and literature for spiritual growth to those we led to Christ at the convention.

I praised God that despite all the tense situations, including the times I felt I was near death, He had not allowed any harm to come to me. I didn't enjoy constantly thinking about death or harm, but it did give me a new perspective on life. I realized, as never before, that not one second can be wasted in working for the Kingdom of God. The premonition of personal disaster changed my whole attitude toward the ministry God had given "God's Love in Action."

While I spoke at a series of meetings in Illinois in August, the rest of the staff went to the Republican National Convention to engage in a ministry similar to the one in July. Tex and I turned our eyes to Europe where we would return for our second step in reaching the world for Jesus.

We'd planned to go back to Germany in September for several months of meetings and rallies. We were anxious to see Murray and Debbie and Volkhardt and the many other friends we'd come to love during our first trip.

God had richly blessed us in every aspect of our outreach, so we knew that He would continue to provide and protect if we would but die to ourselves and become truly alive unto Him.

10 / The World for Jesus

The day before Tex and Davey and I were to leave for Germany, Greg and Lloyd surprised me. They said they felt God leading them into similar ministries of their own in their hometowns. They would not remain to keep our ministry going in Miami. I was thrilled for them and assured them of my prayer support. But I was puzzled too. What was God fixing to do?

The next night, Tex and I looked forward to meeting Murray and Debbie Bradfield at the airport in Luxembourg.

It was tremendous to see Murray and Debbie again. Murray had grown so beautifully in the Lord. Had there been a "God's Love in Action" staff in Miami, Murray would not have been available to head it as we had planned earlier.

"Sam," he told me, "God has impressed so heavily upon me the phrase: 'The world for Jesus.' God has given me a burden for this country and for Europe. I feel He wants me to stay here to minister."

Things were working out beautifully. When Murray and Debbie left to visit the United States for a month, Tex and I found ourselves alone for the first time in our ministry since early in our Chicago days. We had few contacts and still knew very little German. We were alone. We spent the first several days just resting and praying, seeking the will of God.

While praying one day, I felt the Lord impress upon my heart that I should memorize my testimony in German. I didn't understand. Aside from the few times I had witnessed one-to-one on the street, I always had used interpreters when speaking. But the message was clear. I began to memorize, anxiously looking to when God might use me.

During the next several days we had joyous reunions with Don Price, Ricky Auxier, Volkhardt Spitzer, Len Norwicke, and the Schoch family. What blessed times we had, praising God, singing, and praying together!

One night we visited an Evangelical Free church where only German was spoken. The pastor called on various ones to share their testimonies. I was thrilled to hear these German Christians, and it intrigued me that the pastor would call on them, rather than simply let them stand and speak as they felt led.

Suddenly he pointed at me. *"Du!* (You!)" he said. *"Du!"*

Praise God, I thought. I stood and shared my testimony in German as God had directed. It was one of the great blessings of my ministry to be able to share with these people in their own tongue. Not long after, God impressed upon me the need for me to learn Spanish. It puzzles me, but I will obey.

Twice while traveling by train through Germany, I felt God tell me to witness for Him publicly. At one point I could contain myself no longer. I jumped to my feet and shared Christ with those on the train. I sat next to a young man and asked, *"Kennen Sie Jesus?"* (Do you know Jesus?)

"No," he said softly in German, his voice full of terror. "I have been taught that there is no Jesus." This broke my heart. Time and time again I talked with young people, and always their answer was the same. "We have been taught that there is no God." My heart became burdened to share Christ with the untold masses. I could see the hunger for Jesus in their eyes, even as they warned me not to speak publicly of my faith.

Rallies were lined up for us in Walldorf and the surrounding area. During one we ran into some opposition. A gang of youths was there, shouting down our testimonies. Ricky was trying to speak when they began their disruption. God gave me the boldness to confront them. I took the microphone.

"We've not come here to play games!" I said, and the translator echoed the message in German: *Wir sind nicht hier gekommen um Spiele zu spielen!* "We've come here to talk about Jesus (*Wir sind gekommen um uber Jesus zu sprechen*). If you don't want to listen, get out! (*Wenn Sie nicht Zuhoren mochten, gehen Sie hinaus!*)" They respected the boldness the Spirit gave me, and they shut up!

Opportunities began to open for us in the local schools. We would give our testimonies, and the kids then would ask questions. They came up with some real heavy, intellectual questions, but God gave me the wisdom to answer from the Word. Many young people received Christ through those sessions.

A Christian music group asked me to come and speak at a meeting of all the youth workers of evangelical churches in Germany. And through that meeting came many opportunities to share Jesus at rallies and meetings. God opened doors all over Germany.

Murray felt led to minister in the western part of Europe while I felt led to concentrate in the eastern regions. But the New Testament indicates that most ministers of the

Gospel traveled in pairs; so when I felt a call to go to Israel for a few weeks, Murray and I began praying to see if God would have him join me.

I first had felt a tug toward Israel when I had spoken to the students at a Chicago synagogue. But I first felt a definite call to visit there while on a mountain retreat in Germany with several Christian brothers and sisters.

About ten of us prayed and fasted, seeking the will of God for our lives. At one point, we all concentrated on praying about what God would have me do next. One of the brothers was given verses of Scripture which he read aloud to us: "Thine eyes shall see the king in his beauty: they shall behold the land that is very far off" (Isaiah 33: 17); and "Look upon Zion, the city of our solemnities: thine eyes shall see Jerusalem a quiet habitation" (Isaiah 33:20a).

As I prayed, I could almost hear God speaking to my heart. "Go to Jerusalem. Go to Jerusalem. Go to Jerusalem." It was exciting, and I was intrigued by the fact that He was not leading me to the whole nation of Israel, but specifically to Jerusalem. I assumed He would lead me there in the future, so I put it out of my mind for the present.

But two weeks later I couldn't sleep. "Go to Jerusalem" kept echoing in my thoughts. God wanted me to go soon. I got up at 3:00 in the morning and woke Murray. Our wives wondered what was going on. They know that when we get up to pray at 3:00 in the morning, anything can happen.

Murray didn't feel led to go with me at first; but we knew that, if God wanted him to go, He would give us a definite indication. A few days later Murray received a check in the mail from the United States. It was $100, specifically designated for the Holy Land. That paid for a one-way ticket.

About two weeks later, an undesignated check arrived for Murray. It was another $100. On January 2, 1973, we flew to Jerusalem. I half expected to travel about the Holy Land, visiting many places and seeing what God had in store for me. But He wouldn't let us leave Jerusalem. God used those twenty-eight days to teach Murray and me more than we'd ever learned in such a short time.

The first twenty days were spent in constant prayer and Bible study. It was unreal how much the Lord taught us. He instilled in my heart a love for the Scriptures I had never known. He opened the prophetic passages to me so that I understood not only the completeness of the prophecy of Christ's first coming, but of His second coming as well.

Murray and I spent hours at the Garden Tomb, and we made friends with the Dutch warden stationed there. Praying there for hours, I became impressed by God that now, more than ever, the Church needs to be rooted and grounded in the Word of God. Never have I been so convinced that we are living in the last days.

I realized that God wanted me to change the thrust of my ministry somewhat. He told me that I first should teach the Word to the believers and then take them with me into the streets and to public gatherings, rather than just concentrating solely on evangelism. The Body of Christ needs to get back to a scriptural program of instruction and then evangelism.

For days we carried on a spiritual communication in which I was ever reminded that Jesus is coming soon. Hallelujah, praise be to God! My eyes shall behold the King!

On the 6th of January, our wives joined us in Jerusalem.

One day while driving around with Tex, I was taught an invaluable lesson which graphically illustrated the trials of Jesus in His ministry. I got lost and drove into the orthodox section of the city on the Sabbath.

Immediately our rented car was surrounded by angry Jews. They set up human barricades, shouting and banging on the car as I shifted gears furiously, trying to find an exit from the neighborhood. The nerve of anyone to drive a car on the Sabbath! I found out later that they literally might have stoned us, had we not squeaked past them after several minutes. God delivered us from that danger, but only after He had given me a picture of what Jesus went through when He "worked" on the Sabbath. I was shaken by the experience, but I gained incomparable insight.

During our last week in Jerusalem, Murray and I decided to obey Isaiah 62:10, "Go through, go through the gates; prepare ye the way of the people." We felt that God wanted us to walk through each of the seven gates surrounding the city and wind up at the closed gate, the Golden Gate.

The walk was not for publicity or to draw a crowd, so we simply planned to walk through the gates to stand and pray in a secluded spot near each one. We would pray for the future of the Holy City.

We felt the presence of God as we walked through the first gate and prayed and claimed some promises from the Bible. But before we got to the second gate, oh, praise God, the sweet, sweet presence of the Holy Spirit literally drove us to our knees. We found ourselves on that sidewalk, just calling out unto God and asking Him to do something great in Jerusalem. We had a peace and an assurance and a joy in our hearts that God was going to work when we got up from there.

We went through the second gate and got off to the side to pray once again. When we opened our eyes, we found ourselves surrounded by young people. We began to witness to these Muslims, and God poured out His Spirit. One little kid interpreted for us, and we found the crowd hungry to hear about Jesus.

For five days we were blessed with people to witness to. We never approached one person to tell him about Christ. Always, God brought the people to us. It was as if we were in a heavenly situation where God did all the work and we were allowed to share Him the easy way. How many American Christians would love to have God put the listeners in front of them, eager to hear the Gospel?

On the sixth day we had no one to witness to. There was a spiritual battle going on. It was the Sabbath, and over the loud speakers the entire city heard a day-long cry repeated in the Arabic language: "Allah is God! Allah is God! And Muhammad is his prophet! Allah is—" It was eerie.

On Sunday morning the Lord told me that I would be giving my testimony at the Garden Tomb. We had planned to go there for Communion before our last walk; and, when we arrived, we found that the warden, John, wanted to see us. "I want you two to take over the service this morning," he said. "I want you to give your testimonies."

It was a beautiful experience and a thrill to our hearts to share the Lord's Supper and our testimonies with a group of believers in Jerusalem. After the service, we walked to the Golden Gate with a terrific feeling of victory, though no one was led to us to receive our witness.

When we arrived at the Golden Gate, I was overwhelmed with the victorious power of God. Seven times I shouted *"Yeshua Hamashiach!"* (Jesus the Messiah!) At that moment, God wrote on my heart the significance of our walk. He showed me that there will be a long period of worldwide outreach born in prayer, symbolized in our first five days of walking and sharing.

The sixth day symbolized the persecution that the Church will go through after this period of outreach. In saying this I am making no predictions on the Tribulation or anything like that, but I feel certain that a period of effective evangelism will be followed by some form of persecution of the Church.

The last day signified the ultimate victory of Jesus. The Lord convicted me that more and more we need to give ourselves to Bible teaching, preparing the Church for the dark hour and then the eventual victory of Christ.

By the time you read this, I will have been back in the United States for several months. For "God's Love in Action" I foresee a ministry within the local churches, preaching and teaching the Word, preparing the body of believers for evangelism in the marketplace.

Where my study of Spanish will come in, I don't know at this point. We'll be based in San Antonio, Texas, not far from Mexico and Central and South America which may be closed to the Gospel soon. We'll just wait and see what God has for us as we long to be His love in action.

Jesus is coming soon. Hallelujah, praise be to God! My eyes shall behold the King!

JUST BETWEEN YOU AND ME

My goal in serving God has been to die to self so that Jesus Christ can glorify Himself and live His resurrected life in and through me. The aim of this book is not that you see Sammy Tippit, but that you might see Jesus Christ.

In Matthew 10:38-39, Jesus says, "And he that taketh

not his cross, and followeth after me, is not worthy of me. He that findeth his life shall lose it: and he that loseth his life for my sake shall find it."

My hope is that through this book you may be inspired to look daily unto Jesus. Allow Him to fill you with His presence. Let other people see Christ in you.

In Matthew 14:1-2, Jesus says, "At that time Herod the tetrarch heard of the fame of Jesus, and said unto his servants, This is John the Baptist; he is risen from the dead; and therefore mighty works do shew forth themselves in him."

Wow! Can you grasp what the Bible says there? Jesus was mistaken for John the Baptist. John, the one who said, "He must increase, but I must decrease" (John 3:30). Would anyone ever mistake Jesus for you? If Jesus visited a friend of yours, would your friend feel that he'd seen Him before in you? That is my prayer.

If you want to know what spiritual growth is, if you want to know what the Christian life is all about, the answer is in two words: Jesus Christ. Paul said, "For to me to live is Christ" (Philippians 1:21). The secret isn't in witnessing or Bible reading or doing good. The secret is in Jesus Christ.

If you're a Christian and you want to have the abundant life Jesus offers, you must daily die to yourself. Decrease so that Christ may increase in you. The New Testament calls Christ in you the "hope of glory."

When I've tried to live for God on my own, I've blown it. Chaos! Every time. When I have allowed Christ to live His life in me, He has drawn men unto Himself. Learn to put yourself in a casket. Let Christ use you.